Ain't I a Woman

A classic work of feminist scholarship, *Ain't I a Woman* has become a must-read for all those interested in the nature of black womanhood. Examining the impact of sexism on black women during slavery, the devaluation of black womanhood, black male sexism, racism among feminists, and the black woman's involvement with feminism, hooks attempts to move us beyond racist and sexist assumptions. The result is nothing short of groundbreaking, giving this book a critical place on every feminist scholar's bookshelf.

A cultural critic, an intellectual, and a feminist writer, **bell hooks** is best known for classic books including *Feminist Theory, Bone Black, All About Love, Rock My Soul, Belonging, We Real Cool, Where We Stand, Teaching to Transgress, Teaching Community, Outlaw Culture,* and *Reel to Real.* hooks is Distinguished Professor in Residence in Appalachian Studies at Berea College, and resides in her home state of Kentucky.

Ain't I a Woman

BLACK WOMEN AND FEMINISM

bell hooks

Routledge
Taylor & Francis Group

NEW YORK AND LONDON

First published 2015
by Routledge
711 Third Avenue, New York, NY 10017

and by Routledge
2 Park Square, Milton Park, Abingdon, Oxon OX14 4RN

Routledge is an imprint of the Taylor & Francis Group, an informa business

© 2015 Gloria Watkins

First edition published
by South End Press 1981

Library of Congress Cataloging-in-Publication Data

hooks, bell, 1952–
    Ain't I a woman : Black women and feminism / bell hooks. — [Second edition].
        pages cm
    Includes bibliographical references and index.
    1. African American women—Social conditions.   2. Sexism—United States.
3. Feminism—United States.   I. Title.
    E185.86.H73 2014
    305.48′896073—dc23
    2014022890

ISBN: 978-1-138-82148-4 (hbk)
ISBN: 978-1-138-82151-4 (pbk)
ISBN: 978-1-315-74326-4 (ebk)

Typeset in Garamond Premier Pro
by Apex CoVantage, LLC

For Rosa Bell, my mother—

who told me when I was a child that she had once written poems—
that I had inherited my love of reading and my longing to write
from her.

Contents

Preface to the
New Edition

Growing up I knew that I wanted to be a writer. From girlhood on books had offered me visions of new worlds different from the one that was most familiar to me. Like exotic and strange new lands, books brought adventure, new ways to think and be. Most importantly they brought a different perspective, one that almost always forced me out of my comfort zones. I was awed that books could offer a different standpoint, that words on the page could transform and change me, change my mind. During my undergraduate college years, contemporary feminist movement was challenging sexist-defined roles, calling for an end to patriarchy. In those heady days, *women's liberation* was the name given to this amazing new way of thinking about gender. As I had never felt like I had a place in traditional sexist notions of what a female should be and do, I was eager to participate in women's liberation, wanting to create a space of freedom for myself, for the women I loved, for all women.

My intense engagement with feminist consciousness raising compelled me to confront the reality of race, class, and gender difference. Just as I had rebelled against sexist notions of a woman's place, I challenged notions of women's place and identity within women's liberation circles, I could not find a place for myself within the movement. My experience as a young black female was not acknowledged. My voice and the voices of women like me were not heard. Most importantly, the movement had exposed how little I knew about myself, my place in society.

I could not truly belong in the movement so long as I could not make my voice heard. Before I could demand that others listen to me I had to listen to myself, to discover my identity. Taking women's studies courses had shined a spotlight on society's expectations of females. I had learned many new facts about gender differences, about sexism and patriarchy and the ways these systems shaped female roles and identity, but I learned little about the role black females were assigned in our culture. To understand myself as a black female, to understand the place set for black females in this society, I had to explore beyond the classroom, beyond the many treatises and books my fellow white female comrades were creating to explain women's liberation, to offer new and alternative radical ways of thinking about gender and women's place.

To forge a place for black females in this revolutionary movement for gender justice, I had to deepen my understanding of our place in the large society. Even though I was learning so much about sexism and the ways sexist thinking shaped female identity, I was not being taught about the ways race shaped female identity. In classes and in consciousness-raising groups when I called attention to the differences created in our lives by race and racism, I was often treated with disdain by white female comrades who were eager to bond around shared notions of sisterhood. And there I was, this bold young black female from rural Kentucky, insisting that there were major differences shaping the experiences of black and white women. My efforts to understand those differences, to explain and communicate their meaning, lay the groundwork for the writing of *Ain't I a Woman: Black Women and Feminism*.

I began researching and writing during my undergraduate years. It amazes me that more than forty years have passed since I began the work. Initially my search for a publisher led to rejection. In those days no one really imagined there to be an audience for a work about black women. In general, black folks then were far more likely to denounce women's liberation, seeing it as a white woman thing. As a consequence, black female individuals who eagerly embraced the movement were often isolated and estranged from other black folks. We were usually the only black person in predominately white circles. And any talk of race was viewed as shifting the attention away from the politics of gender. No wonder then that black females had to create a separate and distinct body of work that would bring together our understanding of race, class, and gender.

Mating radical feminist politics with my urge to write, I decided early on that I wanted to create books that could be read and understood across different class boundaries. In those days feminist thinkers grappled with the question of audience: who did we want to reach with our work? To reach a broader audience required the writing of work that was clear and concise, that could be read by readers who had never attended college or even finished high school. Imagining my mother as my ideal audience—the reader I most wanted to convert to feminist thinking—I cultivated a way of writing that could be understood by readers from diverse class backgrounds.

Finishing the writing of *Ain't I a Woman*, then years later seeing the work published in my late twenties, marked the culmination of my own struggles to be fully self-actualized, to be a free and independent woman. When I entered my first women's studies class, taught by the white woman writer Tillie Olson, and listened to her talk about the world of women struggling to work and parent, women who were often held captive by male domination, I cried as she cried. We read her seminal work *I Stand Here Ironing* and I began to see my mama and women like her, all raised in the fifties, in a new light. Mama married young, while still in her teens, had babies young, and though she would never have called herself a woman's libber she had experienced the pain of sexist domination, and that led her to encourage all her daughters, all six of us, to educate ourselves so that we would be able to take care of our material and economic needs and never be dependent on any man. Sure we were to find a man and marry, but not before we learned to take care of ourselves. Mama, who was herself held captive by the bonds of patriarchy, encouraged us to break free. It is fitting then that an image of Rosa Bell, my mother, now graces the cover of this new edition.

More than any other book I have written, my relationship to my mother informed the writing of *Ain't I a Woman* and inspired me. Written when contemporary feminist movement was still young, when I was young, this early work has many flaws and imperfections, yet it continues to serve as a powerful catalyst for readers who are eager to explore the roots of black women and feminism. Even though mama has died, no day passes that I do not think of her and all the black women like her, who with no political movement supporting them, no theory of how to be feminist, provided practical blueprints for liberation, offering generations coming after them the gift of choice, freedom, wholeness of mind, body, and being.

Acknowledgments

Eight years ago, when I first began research for this book, discussions of "Black Women and Feminism" or "Racism and Feminism" were uncommon. Friends and strangers were quick to question and ridicule my concern with the lot of black women in the United States. I can remember a dinner where I talked about the book and one person, in a big booming voice choking with laughter exclaimed, "What is there to say about black women!" Others joined the laughter. I had written in the manuscript that the existence of black women was often forgotten, that we were often ignored or dismissed, and my lived experience as I shared the ideas in this book demonstrated the truth of this assertion.

In most stages of my work I had the help and support of Nate, my friend and companion. It was he who said to me when I first returned home from libraries angry and disappointed that there were so few books about black women that I should write one. He also searched for background information and assisted me in a number of ways. A tremendous source of encouragement and support for my work came from fellow black women workers at the Berkeley Telephone Office in 1973-74. When I left there to attend graduate school in Wisconsin, I lost contact with these women. But their energy, their sense that there was much that needed to be said about black women, and their belief that "I" could say it, has sustained me. During the publication process, Ellen Herman of South End Press has been a great help. Our relationship has been political; we have worked to bridge the gap between public and private, making the contact between writer and publisher an affirming experience rather than a de-humanizing one.

This book is dedicated to Rosa Bell Watkins who taught me, and all her daughters, that Sisterhood empowers women by respecting, protecting, encouraging, and loving us.

Introduction

At a time in American history when black women in every area of the country might have joined together to demand social equality for women and a recognition of the impact of sexism on our social status, we were by and large silent. Our silence was not merely a reaction against white women liberationists or a gesture of solidarity with black male patriarchs. It was the silence of the oppressed—that profound silence engendered by resignation and acceptance of one's lot. Contemporary black women could not join together to fight for women's rights because we did not see "womanhood" as an important aspect of our identity. Racist, sexist socialization had conditioned us to devalue our femaleness and to regard race as the only relevant label of identification. In other words, we were asked to deny a part of ourselves—and we did. Consequently, when the women's movement raised the issue of sexist oppression, we argued that sexism was insignificant in light of the harsher, more brutal reality of racism. We were afraid to acknowledge that sexism could be just as oppressive as racism. We clung to the hope that liberation from racial oppression would be all that was necessary for us to be free. We were a new generation

1

of black women who had been taught to submit, to accept sexual inferiority, and to be silent.

Unlike us, black women in 19th century America were conscious of the fact that true freedom entailed not just liberation from a sexist social order that systematically denied all women full human rights. These black women participated in both the struggle for racial equality and the women's rights movement. When the question was raised as to whether or not black female participation in the women's rights movement was a detriment to the struggle for racial equality, they argued that any improvement in the social status of black women would benefit all black people. Addressing the World Congress of Representative Women in 1893, Anna Cooper spoke on the status of black women:

> The higher fruits of civilization cannot be extemporized, neither can they be developed normally in the brief space of thirty years. It requires the long and painful growth of generations. Yet all through the darkest period of the colored women's oppression in this country her yet unwritten history is full of heroic struggle, a struggle against fearful and overwhelming odds, that often ended in a horrible death; to maintain and protect that which woman holds dearer than life. The painful, patient, and silent toil of mothers to gain a fee, simple title to the bodies of their daughters, the despairing fight, as of an entrapped tigress, to keep hallowed their own persons, would furnish material for epics. That more went down under the flood than stemmed the current is not extraordinary. The majority of our women are not heroines—but I do not know that a majority of any race of women are heroines. It is enough for me to know that while in the eyes of the highest tribunal in America she was deemed no more than chattel, an irresponsible thing, a dull block, to be drawn hither or thither at the volition of an owner, the Afro-American woman maintained ideals of womanhood unashamed by any ever conceived. Resting or fermenting in untutored minds, such ideals could not claim a hearing at the bar of the nation. The white woman could at least plead for her own emancipation; the black women doubly enslaved, could but suffer and struggle and be silent.

For the first time ever in American history, black women like

Mary Church Terrell, Sojourner Truth, Anna Cooper, Amanda Berry Smith and others broke through the long years of silence and began to articulate and record their experiences. In particular they emphasized the "female" aspect of their being which caused their lot to be different from that of the black male, a fact that was made evident when white men supported giving black men the vote while leaving all women disenfranchised. Horace Greeley and Wendell Phillips called it "the Negro's hour" but in actuality what was spoken of as black suffrage was black male suffrage. By supporting black male suffrage and denouncing white women's rights advocates, white men revealed the depths of their sexism—a sexism that was at that brief moment in American history greater than their racism. Prior to white male support of suffrage for black men, white women activists had believed it would further their cause to ally themselves with black political activists, but when it seemed black men might get the vote while they remained disenfranchised, political solidarity with black people was forgotten and they urged white men to allow racial solidarity to overshadow their plans to support black male suffrage.

As the racism of white women's rights advocates surfaced, the fragile bond between themselves and black activists was broken. Even though Elizabeth Stanton in her article "Women and Black Men," published in the 1869 issue of the *Revolution*, attempted to show that the republican cry for "manhood suffrage" was aimed at creating antagonism between black men and all women, the break between the two groups could not be mended. While many black male political activists sympathized with the cause of women's rights advocates, they were not willing to lose their own chance to gain the vote. Black women were placed in a double bind; to support women's suffrage would imply that they were allying themselves with white women activists who had publicly revealed their racism, but to support only black male suffrage was to endorse a patriarchal social order that would grant them no political voice. The more radical black women activists demanded that black men and all women be given the vote. Sojourner Truth was the most outspoken black women on this issue. She argued publicly in favor of women gaining the right to vote and emphasized that without this right black women would have to submit to the will of black men. Her famous statement, "there is a great stir about colored men getting their rights, but not a word about the colored woman; and if colored men get their rights, and not colored women theirs, you see the colored men will be masters over the women, and it will be just as bad as it was before," reminded the American public that sexist oppression was as real a threat to the freedom of black women as racial oppression. But despite protests from white and black women activists sexism carried the day and black men received the vote.

Although black women and men had struggled equally for liberation during slavery and much of the Reconstruction era, black male political leaders upheld patriarchal values. As black men advanced in all spheres of American life, they encouraged black women to assume a more subservient role. Gradually the radical revolutionary spirit that had characterized the intellectual and political contribution of black women in the 19th century was quelled. A definite change in the role played by black women in the political and social affairs of black people occurred in the 20th century. This change was indicative of an overall decline in the efforts of all American women to effect radical social reform. When the women's rights movement ended in the twenties, the voices of black women liberationists were stilled. The war had stripped the movement of its earlier fervor. While black women participated equally with black men in the struggle for survival by entering the work force whenever possible, they did not advocate an end to sexism. Twentieth century black women had learned to accept sexism as natural, a given, a fact of life. Had surveys been taken among black women in the thirties and forties and had they been asked to name the most oppressive force in their lives, racism and not sexism would have headed the list.

When the civil rights movement began in the 50s, black women and men again joined together to struggle for racial equality, yet black female activists did not receive the public acclaim awarded black male leaders. Sexist role patterning was as much the norm in black communities as in any other American community. It was an accepted fact among black people that the leaders who were most revered and respected were men. Black activists defined freedom as gaining the right to participate as full citizens in American culture; they were not rejecting the value system of that culture. Consequently, they did not question the rightness of patriarchy. The 60s movement toward black liberation marked the first time black people engaged in a struggle to resist racism in which clear boundaries were erected which separated the roles of women and men. Black male activists publicly acknowledged that they expected black women involved in the movement to conform to a sexist role pattern. They demanded that black women assume a subservient position. Black women were told that they should take care of household needs and breed warriors for the revolution. Toni Cade's article "On the Issue of Roles" is one discussion of the sexist attitudes that prevailed in black organizations during the 60s:

> It would seem that every organization you can name has had to struggle at one time or another with seemingly mutinous cadres of women getting salty about having to man the telephones or fix the coffee while the men wrote the position papers and decided on policy. Some groups condescendingly alloted two or three slots in the executive order to women. Others encouraged the sisters to form a separate caucus and work out something that wouldn't split the organization. Others got nasty and forced the women to storm out to organize separate workshops. Over the years, things have sort of been cooled out. But I have yet to hear a coolheaded analysis of just what any particular group's stand is on the question. Invariably, I hear from some dude that Black women must be supportive and patient so that black men can regain their manhood. The notion of womanhood, they argue—and only if pressed to address themselves to the notion do they think of it or argue—is dependent on his defining his manhood. So the shit goes on.

While some black women activists resisted the attempts of black men to coerce them into playing a secondary role in the movement, others capitulated to male demands for submission. What had begun as a movement to free all black people from racist oppression became a movement with its primary goal the establishment of black male patriarchy. It is not surprising that a movement so concerned with promoting the interests of black men should fail to draw any attention to the dual impact of sexist and racist oppression on the social status of black women. Black women had been asked to fade into the background—to allow the spotlight to shine solely on black men. That the black woman was victimized by sexist and racist oppression was seen as insignificant, for woman's suffering however great could not take precedence over male pain.

Ironically, while the recent women's movement called attention to the fact that black women were dually victimized by racist and sexist oppression, white feminists tended to romanticize the black female experience rather than discuss the negative impact of that oppression. When feminists acknowledge in one breath that black women are victimized and in the same breath emphasize their strength, they imply that though black women are oppressed they manage to circumvent the damaging impact of oppression by being strong—and that is simply not the case. Usually, when people talk about the "strength" of black women they are referring to the way in which they perceive black women coping with oppression. They ignore the reality that to be strong in the face of oppression is not the same as overcoming oppression, that endurance is not to be confused with transformation. Frequently observers of the black female experience confuse these issues. The tendency to romanticize the black female experience that began in the feminist movement was reflected in the culture as a whole. The stereotypical image of the "strong" black woman was no longer seen as dehumanizing, it became the new badge of black female glory. When the women's movement was at its peak and white women were rejecting the role of breeder, burden bearer, and sex object, black women were celebrated for their unique devotion to the task of mothering; for their "innate" ability to bear tremendous burdens; and for their ever-increasing availability as sex object. We appeared to have been unanimously elected to take up where white women were leaving off. They got *Ms.* magazine; we got *Essence.* They got books discussing the negative impact of sexism on their lives; we got books arguing that black women had nothing to gain by women's liberation. Black women were told that we should find our dignity not in liberation from sexist oppression but in how well we could adjust, adapt, and cope. We had been asked to stand up and be congratulated for being "good little women" and then told to sit down and shut up. No one bothered to discuss the way in which sexism operates both independently of and simultaneously with racism to oppress us.

No other group in America has so had their identity socialized out of existence as have black women. We are rarely recognized as a group separate and distinct from black men, or as a present part of the larger group "women" in this culture. When black people are talked about, sexism militates against the acknowledgement of the interests of black women; when women are talked about racism militates against a recognition of black female interests. When black people are talked about the focus tends to be on black *men*; and when women are talked about the focus tends to be on *white* women. No where is this more evident than in the vast body of feminist literature. A case in point is the following passage describing white female reactions to white male support of black male suffrage in the 19th century taken from William O'Neill's book *Everyone Was Brave*:

> Their shocked disbelief that men would so humiliate them by supporting votes for Negroes but not for women demonstrated the limits of their sympathy for black men, even as it drove these former allies further apart.

This passage fails to accurately register the sexual and racial differentiation which together make for the exclusion of black women. In the statement, "their shocked disbelief that men should so humiliate them by supporting votes for Negroes but not for women," the word men in fact refers only to *white* men, the word Negroes refers only to black *men*, and the word women refers only to *white* women. The racial and sexual specificity of what is being referred to is conveniently left unacknowledged or even deliberately suppressed. Another example is from a more recent work by historian Barbara Berg, *The Remembered Gate: Origins of American Feminism*. Berg comments:

... In their fight for the vote, women both ignored and compromised the principles of feminism. The complexities of American society at the turn of the century induced the suffragists to change the basis of their demand for the franchise.

The women Berg refers to are white women yet she never states this. Throughout American history, the racial imperialism of whites has supported the custom of scholars using the term "women" even if they are referring solely to the experience of white women. Yet such a custom, whether practiced consciously or unconsciously, perpetuates racism in that it denies the existence of non-white women in America. It also perpetuates sexism in that it assumes that sexuality is the sole self-defining trait of white women and denies their racial identity. White women liberationists did not challenge this sexist-racist practice; they continued it.

The most glaring example of their support of the exclusion of black women was revealed when they drew analogies between "women" and "blacks" when what they were really comparing was the social status of white women with that of black people. Like many people in our racist society, white feminists could feel perfectly comfortable writing books or articles on the "woman question" in which they drew analogies between "women" and "blacks." Since analogies derive their power, their appeal, and their very reason for being from the sense of two disparate phenomena having been brought closer together, for white women to acknowledge the overlap between the terms "blacks" and "women" (that is the existence of black women) would render this analogy unnecessary. By continuously making this analogy, they unwittingly suggest that to them the term "woman" is synonymous with "white women" and the term "blacks" synonymous with "black men." What this indicates is that there exists in the language of the very movement that is supposedly concerned with eliminating sexist oppression, a sexist-racist attitude toward black women. Sexist-racist attitudes are not merely present in the consciousness of men in American society; they surface in all our ways of thinking and being. All too frequently in the women's movement it was assumed one could be free of sexist thinking by simply adopting the appropriate feminist rhetoric; it was further assumed that identifying oneself as oppressed freed one from being an oppressor. To a very grave extent such thinking prevented white feminists from understanding and overcoming their own sexist-racist attitudes toward black women. They could pay lip-service to the idea of sisterhood and solidarity between women but at the same time dismiss black women.

Just as the 19th century conflict over black male suffrage versus woman suffrage had placed black women in a difficult position, contemporary black women felt they were asked to choose between a black movement that primarily served the interests of black male patriarchs and a women's movement which primarily served the interests of racist white women. Their response was not to demand a change in these two movements and a recognition of the interests of black women. Instead the great majority of black women allied themselves with the black patriarchy they believed would protect their interests. A few black women chose to ally themselves with the feminist movement. Those who dared to speak publicly in support of women's rights were attacked and criticized. Other black women found themselves in limbo, not wanting to ally themselves with sexist black men or racist white women. That black women did not collectively rally against the exclusion of our interests by both groups was an indication that sexist-racist socialization had effectively brainwashed us to feel that our interests were not worth fighting for, to believe that the only option available to us was submission to the terms of others. We did not challenge, question, or critique; we reacted. Many black women denounced women's liberation as "white female foolishness." Others reacted to white female racism by starting black feminist groups. While we denounced male concepts of black macho as disgusting and offensive, we did not talk about ourselves, about being black women, about what it means to be the victims of sexist-racist oppression.

The most notable attempt by black women to articulate their experiences, their attitudes toward woman's role in society, and the impact of sexism on their lives was the anthology *The Black Woman* edited by Toni Cade. The dialogue ended there. The growing demand for literature about women created a market in which almost anything would sell or at least receive some attention. This was particularly the case with literature about black women. The bulk of literature on black women that emerged as a consequence of the demanding market was thoroughly laden with sexist-racist assumptions. Black men who chose to write about black women did so in a predictably sexist manner. Many anthologies appeared with collections of material drawn from the writings of 19th century black women; these works were usually edited by white people. Gerda Lerner, a white women born in Austria, edited *Black Women in White America, A Documentary History* and received a generous grant to aid her scholarshi . While I think that the collection is an important work, it is significant that in our society white women are given grant money to do research on black women but I can find no instance where black women have received funds to research white women's history. Since so much of the anthologized literature on black women emerges from academic circles, where the pressure to publish is omnipresent, I am inclined to wonder if scholars are motivated by a sincere interest in the history of black women or are merely responding to an available market. The tendency to anthologize writings by black women that are already available in other published works has become so much the norm that it causes me to wonder whether or not this trend also reflects an unwillingness on the part of scholars to deal with the black woman in a serious, critical, scholarly fashion. So frequently in the introductions to these works, authors would state that comprehensive studies of the social status of black women were needed but were yet to be written. I often wondered why no one was interested in writing such books. Joyce Ladner's *Tomorrow's Tomorrow* remains the only serious book-length study of the black female experience by a single author to be found on bookstore shelves in the women's section. Occasionally, black women publish articles in journals on racism and sexism but seem reluctant to examine the impact of sexism on the black woman's social status. Black women writers Alice Walker, Audre Lorde, Barbara Smith, and Cellestine Ware have been the most willing to place their writings in a feminist framework.

When Michele Wallace's book *Black Macho and the Myth of the Superwoman* appeared, it was heralded as the definitive feminist book on black women. Gloria Steinem is quoted on the cover as saying:

> What *Sexual Politics* was to the seventies, Michele Wallace's book could be to the eighties. She crosses the sex-race barrier to make every reader understand the political and intimate truths of growing up black and female in America.

Such a quote seems ironic in light of the fact that Wallace could not even discuss the social status of black women without first engaging in a lengthy diatribe about black men and white women. Curiously enough Wallace labels herself a feminist, even though she says very little about the impact of sexist discrimination and sexist oppression on the lives of black women nor does she discuss the relevance of feminism to black women. While the book is an interesting, provocative account of Wallace's personal life that includes a very sharp and witty analysis of the patriarchal impulses of black male activists, it is neigher an important feminist work nor an important work about black women. It is important as a black woman's story. All too often in our society, it is assumed that one can know all there is to know about black people by merely hearing the life story and opinions of one black person. Steinem makes such a narrowminded, and racist, assumption when she suggests that Wallace's book has a similar scope as Kate Millett's *Sexual Politics*. Millett's book is a theoretical, anayltical examination of sexual politics in America that encompasses a discussion of the nature of sex role patterns, a discussion of their historical background, and a discussion of the pervasiveness of patriarchal values in literature. More than five hundred pages in length, it is not autobiographical and is in many ways extremely pedantic. One can only assume that Steinem believes that the American public can be informed about the sexual politics of black people by merely reading a discussion of the 60s black movement, a cursory examination of the role of black women during slavery, and Michele Wallace's life. While I do not wish to denigrate the value of Wallace's work, I believe that it should be placed in a proper context. Usually, a book that is labeled feminist focuses primarily on some aspect of the "woman question." Readers of *Black Macho and the Myth of the Super-woman* were primarily interested in the author's comments about black male sexuality which comprised the main body of her book. Her short critique of the black female slave experience and their characteristic passive acceptance of sexism was largely ignored.

Although the women's movement motivated hundreds of women to write on the woman question, it failed to generate in depth critical analyses of the black female experience. Most feminists assumed that problems black women faced were caused by racism—not sexism. The assumption that we can divorce the issue of race from sex, or sex from race, has so clouded the vision of American thinkers and writers on the "woman" question that most discussions of sexism, sexist oppression, or woman's place in society are distorted, biased, and inaccurate. We cannot form an accurate picture of woman's status by simply calling attention to the role assigned females under patriarchy. More specifically, we cannot form an accurate picture of the status of black women by simply focusing on racial hierarchies.

From the onset of my involvement with the women's movement I was disturbed by the white women's liberationists' insistence that race and sex were two separate issues. My life experience had shown me that the two issues were inseparable, that at the moment of my birth, two factors determined my destiny, my having been born black and my having been born female. When I entered my first women's studies class at Stanford University, in the early 70s, a class taught by a white woman, I attributed the absence of works written by or about black women to the professor having been conditioned as a white person in a racist society to ignore the existence of black women, not to her having been born female. During that time I expressed to white feminists my concern that so few black women were willing to support feminism. They responded by saying that they could understand the black woman's refusal to involve herself in feminist struggle because she was already involved in the struggle to end racism. As I encouraged black women to become active feminists, I was told that we should not become "women's libbers" because racism was the oppressive force in our life—not sexism. To both groups I voiced my conviction that the struggle to end racism and the struggle to end sexism were naturally intertwined, that to make them separate was to deny a basic truth of our existence, that race and sex are both immutable facets of human identity.

When I began the research for *Ain't I A Woman*, my primary intent was to document the impact of sexism on the social status of black women. I wanted to provide concrete evidence to refute the arguments of antifeminists who so loudly proclaimed that black women were not victims of sexist oppression and were not in need of liberation. As the work progressed, I became increasingly aware that I could arrive at a thorough understanding of the black female experience and our relationship to society as a whole only by examining both the politics of racism and sexism from a feminist perspective. The book then evolved into an examination of the impact of sexism on the black woman during slavery, the devaluation of black womanhood, black male sexism, racism within the recent feminist movement, and the black woman's involvement with feminism. It attempts to further the dialogue about the nature of the black woman's experience that began in 19th century America so as to move beyond racist and sexist assumptions about the nature of black womanhood to arrive at the truth of our experience. Although the focus is on the black female, our struggle for liberation has significance only if it takes place within a feminist movement that has as its fundamental goal the liberation of all people.

1

Sexism and the Black Female Slave Experience

In a retrospective examination of the black female slave experience, sexism looms as large as racism as an oppressive force in the lives of black women. Institutionalized sexism—that is, patriarchy—formed the base of the American social structure along with racial imperialism. Sexism was an integral part of the social and political order white colonizers brought with them from their European homelands, and it was to have a grave impact on the fate of enslaved black women. In its earliest stages, the slave trade focused primarily on the importation of laborers; the emphasis at that time was on the black male. The black female slave was not as valued as the black male slave. On the average, it cost more money to buy a male slave than a female slave. The scarcity of workers coupled with the relatively few numbers of black women in American colonies caused some white male planters to encourage, persuade, and coerce immigrant white females to engage in sexual relationships with black male slaves as a means of producing new workers. In Maryland, in the year 1664, the first anti-amalgamation law was passed; it was aimed at curtailing sexual relationships between white women and enslaved black men. One part of the preamble of this document stated:

> That whatsoever freeborn woman shall intermarry with
> any slave, from and after the last day of the present
> assembly, shall serve the masters of such slaves during the
> life of her husband; and that all the issue of such free born
> women, so married shall be slaves as their fathers were.

The most celebrated case of this time was that of Irish
Nell, an indentured servant sold by Lord Baltimore to a southern planter who encouraged her to marry a black man named
Butler. Lord Baltimore, on hearing of the fate of Irish Nell, was
so appalled that white women were either by choice or coercion
co-habiting sexually with black male slaves that he had the law
repealed. The new law stated that the offspring of relationships
between white women and black men would be free. As efforts
on the part of outraged white men to curtail inter-racial relationships between black men and white women succeeded, the
black female slave acquired a new status. Planters recognized
the economic gain they could amass by breeding black slave
women. The virulent attacks on slave importation also led to
more emphasis on slave breeding. Unlike the offspring of
relationships between black men and white women, the offspring of any black slave woman regardless of the race of her
mate would be legally slaves, and therefore the property of the
owner to whom the female slave belonged. As the market value
of the black female slave increased, larger numbers were stolen
or purchased by white slave traders.

White male observers of African culture in the 18th and
19th centuries were astounded and impressed by the African
male's subjugation of the African female. They were not accustomed to a patriarchal social order that demanded not only that
women accept an inferior status, but that they participate
actively in the community labor force. Amanda Berry Smith, a
19th century black missionary, visited African communities
and reported on the condition of African women:

> The poor women of Africa, like those of India, have a hard
> time. As a rule, they have all the hard work to do. They have
> to cut and carry all the wood, carry all the water on their
> heads, and plant all the rice. The men and boys cut and burn

the bush, with the help of the women; but sowing the rice,
and planting the cassava, the women have to do.

You will often see a great, big man walking ahead with
nothing in his hand but a cutlass (as they always carry that
or a spear), and a woman, his wife, coming on behind with
a great big child on her back, and a load on her head.

No matter how tired she is, her lord would not think
of bringing her a jar of water, to cook his supper with, or of
beating the rice, no, she must do that.

The African woman schooled in the art of obedience to a higher
authority by the tradition of her society was probably seen by
the white male slaver as an ideal subject for slavery. As much of
the work to be done in the American colonies was in the area of
hoe-agriculture, it undoubtedly occurred to slavers that the
African female, accustomed to performing arduous work in the
fields while also performing a wide variety of tasks in the
domestic household, would be very useful on the American
plantation. While only a few African women were aboard the
first ships bringing slaves to the new world, as the slave trade
gathered momentum, females made up one-third of the human
cargo aboard most ships. Because they could not effectively
resist capture at the hands of thieves and kidnappers, African
women became frequent targets for white male slavers. Slavers
also used the capture of women important to the tribe, like the
daughter of a king, as a means of luring African men into
situations where they could be easily captured. Other African
women were sold into slavery as punishment for breaking
tribal laws. A woman found guilty of committing an act of
adultery might be sold into bondage.

White male slavers did not regard the African female as a
threat, so often aboard slave ships black women were stored
without being shackled while black men were chained to one
another. The slavers believed their own safety to be threatened
by enslaved African men, but they had no such fear of the
African female. The placing of African men in chains was to
prevent possible uprisings. As white slavers feared resistance
and retaliation at the hands of African men, they placed as
much distance between themselves and black male slaves as
was possible on board. It was only in relationship to the black

female slave that the white slaver could exercise freely absolute power, for he could brutalize and exploit her without fear of harmful retaliation. Black female slaves moving freely about the decks were a ready target for any white male who might choose to physically abuse and torment them. Initially every slave on board the ship was branded with a hot iron. A cat-o'-nine-tails was used by the slavers to lash those Africans that cried out in pain or resisted the torture. Women were lashed severely for crying. They were stripped of their clothing and beaten on all parts of their body. Ruth and Jacob Weldon, an African couple who experienced the horrors of the slave passage, saw "mothers with babes at their breasts basely branded and scarred, till it would seem as if the very heavens might smite the infernal tormentors with the doom they so richly merited." After the branding all slaves were stripped of any clothing. The nakedness of the African female served as a constant reminder of her sexual vulnerability. Rape was a common method of torture slavers used to subdue recalcitrant black women. The threat of rape or other physical brutalization inspired terror in the psyches of displaced African females. Robert Shufeldt, an observer of the slave trade, documented the prevalence of rape on slave ships. He asserts, "In those days many a negress was landed upon our shored already impregnated by someone of the demonic crew that brought her over."

Many African women were pregnant prior to their capture or purchase. They were forced to endure pregnancy without any care given to their diet, without any exercise, and without any assistance during the labor. In their own communities African women had been accustomed to much pampering and care during pregnancy, so the barbaric nature of childbearing on the slave ship was both physically harmful and psychologically demoralizing. Annals of history record that the American slave ship Pongas carried 250 women, many of them pregnant, who were squeezed into a compartment of 16 by 18 feet. The women who survived the initial stages of pregnancy gave birth aboard ship with their bodies exposed to either the scorching sun or the freezing cold. The numbers of black women who died during childbirth or the number of stillborn children will never be known. Black women with children on board the slave ships were ridiculed, mocked, and treated contemptuously by the slaver crew. Often the slavers brutalized children to watch the anguish of their mothers. In their personal account of life aboard a slave ship, the Weldons recounted an incident in which a child of nine months was flogged continuously for refusing to eat. When beating failed to force the child to eat, the captain ordered that the child be placed feet first into a pot of boiling water. After trying other torturous methods with no success, the captain dropped the child and caused its death. Not deriving enough satisfaction from this sadistic act, he then commanded the mother to throw the body of the child overboard. The mother refused but was beaten until she submitted.

The traumatic experiences of African women and men aboard slave ships were only the initial stages of an indoctrination process that would transform the African free human being into a slave. An important part of the slaver's job was to effectively transform the African personality aboard the ships so that it would be marketable as a "docile" slave in the American colonies. The prideful, arrogant, and independent spirit of the African people had to be broken so that they would conform to the white colonizer's notion of proper slave demeanor. Crucial in the preparation of African people for the slave market was the destruction of human dignity, the removal of names and status, the dispersement of groups so that there would exist no common language, and the removal of any overt sign of an African heritage. The methods the slaver used to de-humanize African women and men were various tortures and punishments. A slave might be severely beaten for singing a sad song. When he deemed it necessary, the slaver would slaughter a slave so as to inspire terror in the enslaved onlookers. These methods of terrorization succeeded in forcing African people to repress their awareness of themselves as free people and to adopt the slave identity imposed upon them. Slavers recorded in their log-books that they were sadistically cruel to Africans aboard the slave ships as a way of "breaking them in" or "taming" them. African females received the brunt of this mass brutalization and terrorization not only because they could be victimized via their sexuality but also because they were more likely to work intimately with the white family than the black male. Since the slaver regarded the black woman as a marketable cook, wet nurse, housekeeper, it was crucial that she be so thoroughly terrorized that she would submit passively to the will of white master, mistress, and their children. In order to make his product saleable, the slaver had to ensure that no recalcitrant black female servant would poison a family, kill children, set fire to the house, or resist in any way. The only insurance he could provide was based on his ability to tame the slave. Undoubtedly, the slave ship experience had a tremendous psychological impact on the psyches of black women and men. So horrific was the passage from Africa to America that only those women and men who could maintain a will to live despite their oppressive conditions survived. White people who observed the African slaves as they departed from the ships on American shores noted that they seemed to be happy and joyful. They thought that the happiness of the African slaves was due to their pleasure at having arrived in a Christian land. But the slaves were only expressing relief. They believed no fate that awaited them in the American colonies could be as horrific as the slave ship experience.

Traditionally, scholars have emphasized the impact of slavery on the black male consciousness, arguing that black men, more so than black women, were the "real" victims of slavery. Sexist historians and sociologists have provided the American public with a perspective on slavery in which the most cruel and de-humanizing impact of slavery on the lives of black people was that black men were stripped of their masculinity, which they then argue resulted in the dissolution and overall disruption of any black familial structure. Scholars have argued further that by not allowing black men to assume their traditional patriarchal status, white men effectively emasculated them, reducing them to an effeminate state. Implicit in this assertion is the assumption that the worst that can happen to a man is that he be made to assume the social status of woman. To suggest that black men were de-humanized solely as a result of not being able to be patriarchs implies that the subjugation of black women was essential to the black male's development of a positive self-concept, an idea that only served to support a sexist social order. Enslaved black men were stripped of the patriarchal status that had characterized their social situation in Africa but they were not stripped of their masculinity. Despite all popular arguments that claim black men were figuratively castrated, throughout the history of slavery in America black men were allowed to maintain some semblance of their societally defined masculine role. In colonial times as in contemporary times, masculinity denoted possessing the attributes of strength, virility, vigor, and physical prowess. It was precisely the "masculinity" of the African male that the white slaver sought to exploit. Young, strong, healthy African males were his prime target. For it was by the sale of virile African men "would-be workers" that the white slave trader expected to receive maximum profit return on his investment. That white people recognized the "masculinity" of the black male is evident by the tasks assigned the majority of black male slaves. No annals of history record that masses of black slave men were forced to execute roles traditionally performed exclusively by women. Evidence to the contrary exists, documenting the fact that there were many tasks enslaved African men would not perform because they regarded them as "female" work. If white women and men had really been obsessed by the idea of destroying black masculinity, they could have physically castrated all black men aboard slave ships or they could easily have forced black men to assume "feminine" attire or perform so-called "feminine" tasks. White slaveholders were ambivalent in regards to their treatment of the black male, for while they exploited his masculinity, they institutionalized measures to keep that masculinity in check. Individual black men were castrated by their owners or by mobs but the purpose of such acts was usually to set an example for other male slaves so that they would not resist white authority. Even if enslaved black men had been able to maintain completely their patriarchal status in relationship to enslaved black women, it would not have made the reality of slave life any less tolerable, any less brutal, or any less de-humanizing.

Oppression of black men during slavery has been described as a de-masculinization for the same reason that virtually no scholarly attention has been given to the oppression of black women during slavery. Underlying both tendencies is the sexist assumption that the experiences of men are more important than those of women and that what matters most among the experiences of men is their ability to assert themselves patriarchally. Scholars have been reluctant to discuss the oppression of black women during slavery because of an unwillingness to seriously examine the impact of sexist and racist oppression on their social status. Unfortunately this lack of interest and concern leads them to deliberately minimize the black female slave experience. Although it in no way diminishes the suffering and oppressions of enslaved black men, it is obvious that the two forces, sexism and racism, intensified and magnified the sufferings and oppressions of black women. The area that most clearly reveals the differentiation between the status of male slaves and female slaves is the work area. The black male slave was primarily exploited as a laborer in the fields; the black female was exploited as a laborer in the fields, a worker in the domestic household, a breeder, and as an object of white male sexual assault.

While black men were not forced to assume a role colonial American society regarded as "feminine," black women were forced to assume a "masculine" role. Black women labored in the fields alongside black men, but few if any black men labored as domestics alongside black women in the white household (with the possible exception of butlers, whose status was still higher than that of a maid). Thus, it would be much more accurate for scholars to examine the dynamics of sexist and racist oppression during slavery in light of the masculinization of the black female and not the de-masculinization of the black male. In colonial American society, privileged white women rarely worked in the fields. Occasionally, white female indentured servants were forced to work in the fields as punishment for misdeeds, but this was not a common practice. In the eyes of colonial white Americans, only debased and degraded members of the female sex labored in the fields. And any white woman forced by circumstances to work in the fields was regarded as unworthy of the title "woman." Although enslaved African women had labored in the fields in African communities, there these tasks were seen as an extension of a woman's feminine role. Transplanted African women soon realized that they were seen as "surrogate" men by white male slavers.

On any plantation with a substantial number of female slaves, black women performed the same tasks as black men; they plowed, planted, and harvested crops. On some plantations black women worked longer hours in the fields than black men. Even though it was a widespread belief among white plantation owners that black women were often better workers than their male counterparts, only a male slave could rise to the position of driver or overseer. Given their African heritage, it was easy for enslaved black women to adapt to farm labor in the colonies. Not only was the displaced African man unaccustomed to various types of farm labor, he often saw many tasks as "feminine" and resented having to perform them. In the states where cotton was the main staple to market, harvesting of crops depended heavily on the labor of black females. Although both black women and men labored to pick the ripe cotton, it was believed that the more delicately tapered fingers of the black female made it easier for her to gather the cotton from the pod. White overseers expected black female workers to work as well if not better than their male counterparts. If a black female worker failed to accomplish the amount of work expected of her, she was punished. White men may have discriminated against black women slaves in choosing to allow only males to be drivers or overseers, but they did not discriminate in the area of punishment. Female slaves were beaten as harshly as male slaves. Observers of the slave experience claim that it was common on a plantation to see a black female stripped naked, tied to a stake, and whipped with a hard saw or club.

On large plantations not all black women labored in the fields. They worked as nurses, cooks, seamstresses, washerwomen, and as maids. The popular notion that black slaves working in the white household were automatically the recipients of preferential treatment is not always substantiated by the personal accounts of slaves. House slaves were less subjected to the physical hardships that beset field workers, but they were more likely to suffer endless cruelty and torture because they were constantly in the presence of demanding mistresses and masters. Black females working in close contact with white mistresses were frequently abused for petty offenses. Mungo White, an ex-slave from Alabama, recalled the conditions under which his mother worked:

> Her task was too hard for any one person. She had to serve as maid to Mr. White's daughter, cook for all de hands, spin and card four cuts of thread a day, and den wash. Dere was one hundred and forty-four threads to de cut. If she didn't get all dis done she got fifty lashes dat night.

House slaves complained repeatedly about the stress and strain of being constantly under the surveillance of white owners.

Racist exploitation of black women as workers either in the fields or domestic household was not as de-humanizing and demoralizing as the sexual exploitation. The sexism of colonial white male patriarchs spared black male slaves the humiliation of homosexual rape and other forms of sexual assault. While institutionalized sexism was a social system that protected black male sexuality, it (socially) legitimized sexual exploitation of black females. The female slave lived in constant awareness of her sexual vulnerability and in perpetual fear that any male, white or black, might single her out to assault and victimize. Linda Brent in the narrative of her slave experience expressed her awareness of the black female's plight:

> Slavery is terrible for men; but it is far more terrible for women. Superadded to the burden common to all, they have wrongs, and suffering, and mortifications peculiarly their own.

Those sufferings peculiar to black women were directly related to their sexuality and involved rape and other forms of sexual assault. Black female slaves were usually sexually assaulted when they were between the ages of thirteen and sixteen. One female slave autobiographer declared:

> The slave girl is reared in an atmosphere of licentiousness and fear. The lash and the foul talk of her masters and his sons are her teachers. When she is fourteen or fifteen, her

owner or his sons, or the overseer, or perhaps all of them, begin to bribe her with presents. If these failed to accomplish their purpose, she is whipped or starved into submission to their will.

Black female slave narratives that provide information concerning the sexual education of girls suggest that they knew little about their bodies, where babies came from, or about sexual intercourse. Few slave parents warned their daughters about the possibility of rape or helped them to prepare for such situations. The slave parents' unwillingness to openly concern themselves with the reality of sexual exploitation reflects the general colonial American attitude regarding sexuality.

Sexual exploitation of young slave girls usually occurred after they left the hut or cabin of their parents to work in the white domestic household. It was a common practice for a young slave girl to be forced to sleep in the same bedroom with a master and mistress, a situation which provided a convenient setting for sexual assault. Linda Brent recorded in her autobiography a detailed account of her white master's obsessive desire to assert his power over her by constantly threatening rape. When Linda first entered the service of her owner Dr. Flint, she was thirteen years old. He did not rape her but began to constantly torment and persecute her by verbally announcing his intentions to take her sexually. At the onset of their encounter he informed her that if she would not willingly submit, he would use force. Describing herself at fifteen, Linda wrote:

> I was compelled to live under the same roof with him—where I saw a man forty years my senior daily violating the most sacred commandment of nature. He told me I was his property; that I must be subjected to his will in all things...

White male slaveowners usually tried to bribe black women as preparation for sexual overtures so as to place them in the role of prostitute. As long as the white slaveowner "paid" for the sexual services of his black female slave, he felt absolved of responsibility for such acts. Given the harsh conditions of slave life, any suggestion that enslaved black women had a choice as to their sexual partner is ludicrous. Since the white male could rape the black female who did not willingly respond to his demands, passive submission on the part of the enslaved black women cannot be seen as complicity. Those women who did not willingly respond to the sexual overture of masters and overseers were brutalized and punished. Any show of resistance on the part of enslaved females increased the determination of white owners eager to demonstrate their power. In an account of her slave experience, Ann, a young mulatto woman, documents the struggle for power enacted by white masters, overseers, whippers, and the female slave. In her case it was the paid whipper who planned to rape her. He demanded that she remove all her clothing prior to the whipping. When Ann realized that he intended to rape her, she struggled. Her resistence angered him and he responded, "Girl, you've got to yield to me. I'll have you now; if it's only to show you that I can...You've got to be mine. I'll give you a fine calico dress and a pretty pair of ear-bobs!" Ann tells readers:

> This was too much for further endurance. What! Must I give up the angel sealed honor of my life in traffic for trinkets. Where is the woman that would not have hotly resented such an insult. I turned upon him like a hungry lioness, and just as his wanton hand was about to be laid upon me, I dexterously aimed, and hurled the bottle against his left temple. With a low cry of pain he fell to the floor, and the blood oozed freely from the wound.

The paid whipper did not die from Ann's attack, so she was only punished by a prison sentence and daily floggings. Had he died she would have been tried for murder and sentenced to death.

Nineteenth century white female humanist Lydia Marie Child accurately summed up the social status of black women during slavery with the statement:

> The negro woman is unprotected either by law or public opinion. She is the property of her master, and her daughters are his property. They are allowed to have no conscientious scruples, no sense of shame, no regard for the feelings of husband, or parent: they must be entirely subservient to the will of their owner on pain of being whipped as near unto death as will comport with his interest or quite to death if it suits his pleasure.

White male slaveowners wanted enslaved black women to passively accept sexual exploitation as the right and privilege of those in power. The black female slave who willingly submitted to a master's sexual advance and who received presents of payments was rewarded for her acceptance of the existing social order. Those black women who resisted sexual exploitation directly challenged the system; their refusal to submit passively to rape was a denouncement of the slaveowner's right to their persons. They were brutally punished. The political aim of this categorical rape of black women by white males was to obtain absolute allegiance and obedience to the white imperialistic order. Black activist Angela Davis has convincingly argued that the rape of black female slaves was not, as other scholars have suggested, a case of white men satisfying their sexual lust, but was in fact an institutionalized method of terrorism which had as its goal the demoralization and dehumanization of black women. Davis contends:

> In confronting the black woman as adversary in a sexual contest, the master would be subjecting her to the most elemental form of terrorism distinctly suited for the female: rape. Given the already terroristic texture of plantation life, it would be as potential victim of rape that the slave woman would be most unguarded. Further, she might be most conveniently manipulated if the master contrived a random system of sorts, forcing her to pay with her body for foods, diminished severity of treatment, the safety of her children, etc.

In 1839, the book *American Slavery: As It Is* was published anonymously by white abolitionists who believed they could destroy the pro-slavery arguments by exposing in print the horrors of slave life. They relied on the accounts of white people who had observed slavery firsthand or had gained information from slaveholders and their friends. The work was compiled and collated primarily by Angelina and Sarah Grimke, two outspoken abolitionists. Because their brother had fathered children by a black female slave, they were particularly concerned about the sexual exploitation of black female slaves. For many other white female abolitionists the sole motivating force behind their anti-slavery efforts was the desire to bring an end to sexual contact between white men and black female slaves. They were not concerned about the plight of enslaved black women, but about saving the souls of white men whom they believed had sinned against God by their acts of moral depravity. Many pro-slavery white women ultimately denounced slavery because of their outrage at the sexual barbarity of white men. They felt personally shamed and humiliated by what they termed white male adultery (which was in actuality rape). Commenting on her mistress' attitude toward the sexual exploitation of black women, Linda Brent wrote:

> I was soon convinced that her emotions arose from anger and wounded pride. She felt that her marriage vows were desecrated, her dignity insulted; but she had no compassion for the poor victim of her husband's perfidy. She pitied herself as a martyr; but she was incapable of feeling for the condition of shame and misery in which her unfortunate, helpless slaves were placed.

The Grimke women sympathized with the plight of black females but Victorian social convention governing behavior did not allow them to graphically expose many of the cruel acts inflicted upon black slave women by white men. Proper decorum prevented them from speaking directly and honestly about the hidden evils of slavery. Angelina Grimke wrote:

> We forbear to lift the veil of private life any higher. Let these few hints suffice to give you some idea of what is daily passing behind the curtain which has been so carefully drawn before the scenes of domestic life in slave holding America.

Had Angelina and Sarah Grimke lifted the veil of private life any higher they would have exposed not only slaveowners siring children by black women, but sadistic misogynist acts of cruelty and brutality that went far beyond seduction—to rape, to torture, and even to orgiastic murder and necrophilia.

Modern historians tend to make light of the sexual exploitation of black women during slavery. In his *Daughters of the Promised Land* Page Smith writes:

> Most young Southern men doubtless had their initial sexual experience with a compliant slave girl. It was not

unnatural that many of them should continue to indulge themselves after their marriages. In addition there was undoubtedly the attraction of the perverse, of the taboo, the association of darkness with pleasant wickedness, the absence of any danger to the sexual exploiter however unwelcome his attentions may have been. Moreover, there was the tradition of Negro sensuality which may well have worked to make the white wife a more restrained sexual partner. Thus when the Southern male looked to slave women for his basic sexual satisfaction, he increasingly found them there. Since there seems to be in masculine sexuality a measure of aggressiveness and even sadism, passivity and defenselessness seem often to enhance the desirability of the sexual object which was what the Negro woman was for her white masters.

The reader is encouraged by Smith to regard the brutality of white men as merely a case of "boys will be boys." Like many other historians, he paints a picture of slavery in which white men had "normal" male sexual desires that they indulged with submissive slave girls. While he acknowledges the sadism that often prompted sexual exploitation of the black female slave, he minimizes it by implying that it was an extension of "normal" male sexual expression.

The brutal treatment of enslaved black women by white men exposed the depths of male hatred of woman and woman's body. Such treatment was a direct consequence of misogynist attitudes toward women that prevailed in colonial American society. In fundamentalist Christian teaching woman was portrayed as an evil sexual temptress, the bringer of sin into the world. Sexual lust originated with her and men were merely the victims of her wanton power. Socialization of white men to regard women as their moral downfall led to the development of anti-woman sentiment. White male religious teachers taught that woman was an inherently sinful creature of the flesh whose wickedness could only be purged by the intercession of a more powerful being. Appointing themselves as the personal agents of God, they became the judges and overseers of woman's virtue. They instigated laws to govern the sexual behavior of white women, to ensure that they would not be tempted to stray from the straight and narrow path. Severe punishments were meted out to those women who overstepped the boundaries white men defined as woman's place. The Salem Witchcraft trials were an extreme expression of patriarchal society's persecution of women. They were a message to all women that unless they remained within passive, subordinate roles they would be punished, even put to death.

The numerous laws enacted to govern sexual behavior among early American whites have caused some scholars to conclude that the movement toward sexual repression in colonial society occurred as a reaction against the sexual permissiveness of the colonizers. Andrew Sinclair comments:

> The terrible liberty of isolation and the wilderness made some of the first settlers discard their European moral restraints. Cases of bestiality, according to Cotton Mather, were not unknown.... As the first missionaries of the West were told, barbarism was the first danger to the pioneers, 'They will think it no degradation to do before the woods and wild animals, what, in the presence of a cultivated social state they would blush to perpetrate.' Until a stern public opinion could govern the ethics of a scattered and immigrant society, small governments tried to do what they could to keep up the standards of civilization.

White colonizers sought to suppress sexuality because of their deep fear of sexual feelings, their belief that such feelings were sinful, and their fear of eternal damnation. Colonial white men placed the responsibility for sexual lust onto women and consequently regarded them with the same suspicion and distrust they associated with sexuality in general. Such intense fear and distrust of women bred misogynistic feeling. In the *Troublesome Helpmate*, Katherine Rogers offers an explanation for the emergence of misogynic feeling:

> Of the cultural causes of misogyny, rejection of or guilt about sex is the most obvious. It leads naturally to degradation of woman as the sexual object and projection onto her of the lust and desire to seduce which a man must repress in himself. At the same time that he denigrated woman's sexual function, the preoccupation with sex resulting from the attempt to repress desire is apt to make him see her exclusively as a sexual being, more lustful than man and not spiritual at all....

> Misogyny can also develop as a result of the idealiza-
> tion with which men have glorified women as mistresses,
> wives, and mothers. This has led to a natural reaction, a
> desire to tear down what has been raised unduly high.

Colonial white men expressed their fear and hatred of womanhood by institutionalizing sexist discrimination and sexist
oppression.

In the 19th century, the growing economic prosperity of
white Americans caused them to stray from the stern religious
teachings that had shaped the life of the first colonizers. With
the shift away from fundamentalist Christian doctrine came a
change in male perceptions of women. 19th century white
women were no longer portrayed as sexual temptresses; they
were extolled as the "nobler half of humanity" whose duty was
to elevate men's sentiments and inspire their higher impulses.
The new image of white womanhood was diametrically
opposed to the old image. She was depicted as goddess rather
than sinner; she was virtuous, pure, innocent, not sexual and
wordly. By raising the white female to a goddess-like status,
white men effectively removed the stigma Christianity had
placed on them. White male idealization of white women as
innocent and virtuous served as an act of exorcism, which had
as its purpose transforming her image and ridding her of the
curse of sexuality. The message of the idealization was this: as
long as white women possessed sexual feeling they would be
seen as degraded immoral creatures; remove those sexual feelings and they become beings worthy of love, consideration, and
respect. Once the white female was mythologized as pure and
virtuous, a symbolic Virgin Mary, white men could see her as
exempt from negative sexist stereotypes of the female. The
price she had to pay was the suppression of natural sexual
impulses. Given the strains of endless pregnancies and the
hardships of childbirth, it is understandable that 19th century
white women felt no great attachment to their sexuality and
gladly accepted the new, glorified de-sexualized identity white
men imposed upon them. Most white women eagerly absorbed
sexist ideology that claimed virtuous women had no sexual
impulses. So convinced were they of the necessity to hide their
sexuality that they were unwilling to undress to expose sick

body parts to male physicians. A French visitor to America observed, "American women divide their whole body in two parts; from the top to the waist is the stomach; from there to the foot is ankles." On this same subject Page Smith comments:

> They were too modest to let a doctor touch their bodies and they could not even bring themselves, in some instances, to describe an ailment, like one young mother with an ulcerated breast who, too prudish to speak frankly to the doctor, described her condition as a pain in the stomach.

Forcing white women to deny their physical beings was as much an expression of male hatred of woman as was regarding them as sex objects. Idealization of white women did not change the basic contempt white men felt towards them. Visitors from foreign countries often noticed the veiled hostility of white men towrds white women. One visitor commented:

> American men accorded their women more deference, lavished more money on them, regarded them with more respect than was accorded the women of any country. But they did not particularly like them. They did not enjoy their company; they did not find them interesting in themselves. They valued them as wives and mothers, they sentimentalized over them; they congratulated themselves on their enlightened attitude toward them. But they did not (and they do not) particularly like them.

The shift away from the image of white woman as sinful and sexual to that of white woman as virtuous lady occurred at the same time as mass sexual exploitation of enslaved black women—just as the rigid sexual morality of Victorian England created a society in which the extolling of woman as mother and helpmeet occurred at the same time as the formation of a mass underworld of prostitution. As American white men idealized white womanhood, they sexually assaulted and brutalized black women. Racism was by no means the sole cause of many cruel and sadistic acts of violence perpetrated by white men against enslaved black women. The deep hatred of woman that had been embedded in the white colonizer's psyche by patriarchal ideology and anti-woman religious teachings both motivated and sanctioned white male brutality against black women. At the onset of their arrival in the American colonies, black women and men faced a society that was eager to impose upon the displaced African the identity of "sexual savage." As white colonizers adopted a self-righteous sexual morality for themselves, they even more eagerly labeled black people sexual heathens. Since woman was designated as the originator of sexual sin, black women were naturally seen as the embodiment of female evil and sexual lust. They were labeled jezebels and sexual temptresses and accused of leading white men away from spiritual purity into sin. One white politician urged that blacks be sent back to Africa so that white men would not fornicate or commit adultery. His words were "remove this temptation from us." Although religious white women, white men, and black men argued that white men were morally responsible for sexual assaults on black women, they tended to accept the notion that men succumb to female sexual temptation. Because sexist religious doctrines had taught them that women were the seducers of men, they believed black women were not totally blameless. Frequently, they used the term "prostitution" to refer to the buying and selling of black women for sexually exploitative purposes. Since prostitutes are women and men who engage in sexual behavior for money or pay of some kind, it is a term inaccurately used when applied to enslaved black women who rarely received compensation for the use of their bodies as sexual latrines. Abolitionist women and men labeled black women "prostitutes" because they were trapped by the language of the Victorian ethos. In speaking of the mass sexual abuse of black women, noted black orator Frederick Douglass told an abolitionist audience in Rochester, New York in 1850 that "every slaveholder is the legalized keeper of a house of ill-fame." Yet his words did not begin to accurately describe the sexual exploitation of black women. Douglass informed his audience:

> I hold myself ready to prove that more than a million of women, in the Southern States of this Union, are, by laws of the land, and through no fault of their own, consigned to a life of revolting prostitution; that by those laws, in many of the States, if a woman, in defense of her own innocence, shall lift her hand against the brutal aggressor, she may be lawfully put to death... It is also known that slave women,

who are nearly white, are sold in those markets, at prices which proclaim, trumpet-tongued, the accursed purposes by which they are to be devoted. Youth and elegance, beauty and innocence, are exposed for sale upon the auction block; while villainous monsters stand around, with pockets lined with gold, gazing with lustful eyes upon their prospective victims.

It was difficult for abolitionists to discuss the rape of black women for fear of offending audiences, so they concentrated on the theme of prostitution. But the use of the word prostitution to describe mass sexual exploitation of enslaved black women by white men not only deflected attention away from the prevalence of forced sexual assault, it lent further credibility to the myth that black females were inherently wanton and therefore responsible for rape.

Contemporary sexist scholars minimize the impact of sexual exploitation of black women on the black female psyche and argue that white men used the rape of black women to further emasculate black men. Black sociologist Robert Staples asserts:

> The rape of the slave woman brought home to the slave man his inability to protect his woman. Once his masculinization was undermined in this respect, he would begin to experience profound doubts about his power even to break the chains of bondge.

Staples' argument is based on the assumption that enslaved black men felt responsible for all black women and were demoralized because of their inability to act as protectors—an assumption that has not been substantiated by historical evidence. An examination of many traditional African societies' attitudes toward women reveals that African men were not taught to see themselves as the protectors of all women. They were taught to assume responsibility for the particular women of their tribe or community. The socialization of African men to see themselves as the "owners" of all black women and to regard them as property they should protect occurred after the long years of slavery and as the result of bonding on the basis of color rather than shared tribal connection or language. Prior to their adoption of white American sexist attitudes toward women, there was no reason for enslaved African men to feel responsible for all enslaved African women. Assuredly, the sexual assault of black women had an impact on the psyches of black male slaves. It is likely that the black male slave did not feel demoralized or de-humanized because "his" women were being raped, but that he did feel terrorized by the knowledge that white men who were willing to brutalize and victimize black women and girls (who represented no great threat to their authority), might easily have no qualms about totally annihilating black men. Most black male slaves stood quietly by as white masters sexually assaulted and brutalized black women and were not compelled to act as protectors. Their first instincts were toward self-preservation. In her slave narrative, Linda Brent tells readers that black male slaves as a group did not see themselves as the protectors of black slave women. She comments:

> There are some who strive to protect wives and daughters from the insults of their master; but those who have such sentiments have advantages above the general mass of slaves... Some poor creatures have been so brutalized by the lash that they will sneak out of the house to give their masters free access to their wives and daughters.

Throughout the years of slavery, individual black men rallied to the defense of black women who were important to them. Their defense of these women was not motivated by a sense of themselves as the natural protectors of all black women.

Historian Eugene Genovese discusses the sexual exploitation of enslaved black females in *Roll, Jordan, Roll*, and contends:

> Rape meant, by definition, rape of white women, for no such crime as rape of a black woman existed at law. Even when a black man sexually attacked a black woman, he could only be punished by his master; no way existed to bring him to trial or to convict him if so brought.

The rape of black women by black male slaves is further indication that, rather than assuming the role of protector, black men imitated the white male's behavior. Genovese concludes:

Some drivers forced the slave woman in much the same way as did some masters and overseers. It remains an open question which of those powerful white and black males forced the female slaves more often. Under the task system the driver set the day's work for each slave and had no trouble making a woman's lot miserable if she refused him. Under the more prevalent gang system, drivers could lay the whip on with impunity—if they had the power to whip at all—as many did—or they could find any number of other ways to reward and punish.

Given the barbaric nature of slave life, it is likely that black slave women allied with powerful black men who could protect them from the unwanted sexual advances of other slaves. Sexual jealousies and rivalries were a primary cause of most quarrels between black slave men.

The enslaved black woman could not look to any group of men, white or black, to protect her against sexual exploitation. Often in desperation, slave women attempted to enlist the aid of white mistresses, but these attempts usually failed. Some mistresses responded to the distress of female slaves by persecuting and tormenting them. Others encouraged the use of black women as sex objects because it allowed them respite from unwanted sexual advances. In rare cases, white mistresses who were reluctant to see sons marry and leave home purchased black maids to be sexual playmates for them. Those white women who deplored the sexual exploitation of slave women were usually reluctant to involve themselves with a slave's plight for fear of jeopardizing their own position in the domestic household. Most white women regarded black women who were the objects of their husbands' sexual assaults with hostility and rage. Having been taught by religious teachings that women were inherently sexual temptresses, mistresses often believed that the enslaved black woman was the culprit and their husbands the innocent victims. In *Once A Slave*, a book which contains a condensed body of information gleaned from slave narratives, the author Stanley Feldstein recounts an incident in which a white mistress returned home unexpectedly from an outing, opened the doors of her dressing room, and discovered her husband raping a thirteen year old slave girl. She responded by beating the girl and locking her in a smokehouse. The girl was whipped daily for several weeks. When older slaves pleaded on the child's behalf and dared to suggest that the white master was to blame, the mistress simply replied, "She'll know better in future. After I've done with her, she'll never do the like again through ignorance." White women held black slave women responsible for rape because they had been socialized by 19th century sexual morality to regard woman as sexual temptress. This same sexual morality was adopted by slaves. Fellow slaves often pitied the lot of sexually exploited females but did not see them as blameless victims. One female abolitionist states:

> Of all who drooped and withered under the inflictions of this horrible system, the greatest sufferer was defenseless women. For the male slave, however brutally treated, there was some recourse; but for the woman slave there was neither protection nor pity.

Rape was not the only method used to terrorize and de-humanize black women. Sadistic floggings of naked black women were another method employed to strip the female slave of dignity. In the Victorian world, where white women were religiously covering every body part, black women were daily stripped of their clothing and publicly whipped. Slave-owners were well aware that it added to the degradation and humiliation of female slaves for them to be forced to appear naked before male whippers and onlookers. A Kentucky slave recalled:

> The women are subjected to these punishments as rigorously as the men—not even pregnancy exempts them; in that case before binding them to the stake, a hole is made in the ground to accomodate the enlarged form of the victim.

Susan Boggs recalled:

> They would have a woman stripped and cobbed if she did anything they didn't like. Perhaps if the bread did not rise well, the mistress would tell the master when he came home; and she would be sent to the trader's jail to be cobbed. It is awful to think of women, of human beings, being exposed in this way.

Sadistic floggings of nude black women were socially sanctioned because they were seen as racial abuse, a master punishing a recalcitrant slave, but they were also expressions of male contempt and hatred for the female. Solomon Bradley, an ex-slave, told a journalist who interviewed him:

> Yes, sir; the most shocking thing that I have seen was on the plantation of Mr. Farrarby, on the line of the railroad. I went up to his house one morning from my work for drinking water, and heard a woman screaming awfully. On going up to the fence and looking over I saw a woman stretched out, face downwards, on the ground her hands and feet being fastened to stakes. Mr. Farrarby was standing over her and striking her with a leather trace belonging to his carriage harness. As he struck her the flesh of her back and legs were raised in welts and ridges by the force of blows. Sometimes when the poor thing cried too loud from the pain Farrarby would kick her in the mouth. After he exhausted himself whipping her he sent to his house for sealing wax and a lighted candle and, melting the wax, dropped it upon the woman's lacerated back. He then got a riding whip and, standing over the woman, picked off the hardened wax by switching at it. Mr. Farrarby's grown daughters were looking at this from a window of the house through the blinds. This punishment was so terrible that I was induced to ask what offence the woman had committed and was told by her fellow servants that her only crime was in burning the edges of the waffles that she had cooked for breakfast.

It takes little imagination to comprehend the significance of one oppressed black woman being brutally tortured while the more privileged white women look passively at her plight. Incidents of this nature exposed to white women the cruelty of their husbands, fathers, and brothers and served as a warning of what might be their fate should they not maintain a passive stance. Surely, it must have occurred to white women that were enslaved black women not available to bear the brunt of such intense anti-women male aggression, they themselves might have been the victims. In most slaveholding homes, white women played as active a role in physical assaults of black women as did white men. While white women rarely physically assaulted black male slaves, they tortured and persecuted black females. Their alliance with white men on the common ground of racism enabled them to ignore the anti-woman impulse that also motivated attacks on black women.

Breeding was another socially legitimized method of sexually exploiting black women. I mentioned earlier that white men in colonial America defined the primary function of all women to be that of breeding workers. Contemporary scholars often dismiss the breeding of slave women on the basis that it occurred on such a small scale as to not merit attention. Yet a rather convincing body of evidence exists substantiating not only the existence of slave breeding but the fact that it was a widespread and common practice. Reporting on the slave trade in the state of Virginia in 1819 Frances Corbin wrote, "Our principal profit depends on the increase of our slaves." During the early years of slavery, breeding of African women was a difficult process. In traditional African communities black women suckled their children at their breasts and weaned them at the late age of two years old. For this time period, the African woman did not engage in sexual intercourse and consequently spaced her pregnancies. This practice allowed women time to recuperate physically before starting a new pregnancy. White slaveowners could not understand the reasons slave women did not bear many children consecutively. Their response to this situation was to use threats of violence as a means of coercing slave women to reproduce. Frederick Olmstead, a southern white observer of the practice of slave breeding, made this comment:

> In the states of Maryland, Virginia, North Carolina, Kentucky, Tennessee, as much attention is paid to the breeding and growth of negroes as to that of horses and mules. Further south, we raise them both for use and for market. Planters command their girls and women (married or unmarried) to have children; and I have known a great many girls to be sold off because they did not have children. A breeding woman is worth from one-sixth to one-fourth more than one that does not breed.

Advertisements announcing the sale of black female slaves used the terms "breeding slaves," "child-bearing woman," "breeding period," "too old to breed," to describe individual women. Moncure Conway, the son of a Virginia slaveholder, recalled:

> As a general thing, the chief pecuniary resource in the border states is the breeding of slaves; and I grieve to say that there is too much ground for the charges that general licentiousness among the slaves for the purpose of a large increase is compelled by some masters and encouraged by many. The period of maternity is hastened, the average youth of negro mothers being nearly three years earlier than that of any free race, and an old maid is utterly known among the women.

Slave women who refused to choose a man and mate with him had men forced upon them by their overseer or master. Some slaveholders preferred to breed black women with white men, as mulattoes frequently brought a higher price on the market or were easier to sell. In a letter dated March 13, 1835 a Methodist minister residing in Virginia observed:

> Mulattoes are surer than pure negroes. Hence planters have no objection to any white man or boy having free intercourse with all the females; and it has been the case that an overseer has been encouraged to make the whole posse his harem and has been paid for the issue.

Barren black women suffered most under the breeding system. In a report presented to the General Anti-Slavery Convention held in London, June 1840, witnesses testified that barren black females were the victims of great physical and psychological abuse. The report stated:

> Where fruitfulness is the greatest of virtues, barrenness will be regarded as worse than a misfortune, as a crime and the subjects of it will be exposed to every form of privation and affliction. Thus a deficiency, wholly beyond the slave's power becomes the occasion of inconceivable suffering.

In this same report, a North Carolina citizen repeated a story told to him by a friend about slave breeding on Carolina plantations.

> One day the owner ordered the women into the barn; he then went in among them, whip in hand, and told them he meant to flog them all to death. They began immediately to cry out, 'What have I done massa? What have I done?' He

replied, 'Damn you, I will let you know what you have done; you don't breed, I have not had a young one from one of you for several months.' "

Some slave owners devised a system of rewards to induce women to breed. But such rewards were rarely commensurate with services rendered. On some plantations a woman might be given a small pig each time a child was born to her. Women were promised a new dress or a new pair of shoes at the birth of a child. A small monetary sum, from one to five dollars, might be given a slave woman at the birth of her fourth or fifth child. A few slaveowners promised freedom to black women who bore large families. A case appeared before the Virginia courts in 1761 in a dispute over a will that included a provision to free a female slave Jenny if she bore ten live children. Some enslaved women desired pregnancy, for they saw it as a means of obtaining certain advantages, the primary one being a lightening of the work load. Frances Kemble in her *Journal of a Residence on a Georgian Plantation in 1838-1839* surmised:

> On the birth of a child certain additions of clothing and an additional weekly ration are bestowed on the family; and these matters small as they may seem, acted as powerful inducements to creatures who have not of the restraining influence activating them which belongs to the parental relation among all other people, whether civilized or savage. Moreover, they have all of them a most distinct and perfect knowledge of their value to their owner as property; and a woman thinks, and not so much amiss that the more frequently she adds to the number of her master's livestock by bringing new slaves into the world, the more claims she will have upon his consideration and good will.

Breeding was oppressive to all fertile black slave women. Undernourished, overworked women were rarely in a physical condition that would allow for safe easy childbirth. Repeated pregnancies without proper care resulted in numerous miscarriages and death. Frances Kemble gave the following account of the condition of black women on her husband's plantation, women who considered themselves well off compared to slaves on neighboring plantations:

> Fanny has had six children; all dead but one, she came to

beg to have her work in the field lightened.

Nanny has had three children; two of them are dead. She came to implore that the rule of sending them into the field three weeks after their confinement might be altered.

Leah, Caesar's wife, has had six children; three are dead.

Sophy, Lewis's wife, came to beg for some old line. She is suffering fearfully; has had ten children; five of them all dead. The principal favor she asked was a piece of meat, which I gave her.

Sally, Scipio's wife, has had two miscarriages and three children born, one of whom is dead. She came complaining of incessant pain and weakness in her back. This woman was a mullatto daughter of a slave called Sophy, by a white man of the name of Walker who visited the plantation.

Charlotte, Renty's wife, has had two miscarriages, and was with child again. She was almost crippled with rheumatism, and showed me a pair of poor swollen knees that made my heart ache. I have promised her a pair of flannel trousers, which I must forthwith set about making.

Sarah, Stephen's wife; this woman's case and history alike are deplorable. She has had four miscarriages, had brought seven children into the world, five of whom were dead, and was again with child. She complained of dreadful pains in the back, and an internal tumor which swells with the exertion of working in the fields; probably I think, it is ruptured.... I suppose her constant childbearing and hard labor in the fields at the same time may have produced... temporary insanity...

I ask these questions about their children because I think the number they bear as compared with the number they rear a fair gauge of the effect of the system on their own health and that of their offspring. There was hardly one of these, as you will see by the details I have noted of their ailments, who might not have been a candidate for a bed in a hospital, and they had come to me after working all day in the fields.

Kemble admired the patience with which suffering enslaved black women endured their harsh lot, but she was not unaware of the "utter despair" that was often masked by their quiet acceptance.

Mass sexual exploitation of enslaved black women was a direct consequence of the anti-woman sexual politics of colonial patriarchal America. Since the black woman was not protected either by law or public opinion, she was an easy target. While racism was clearly the evil that had decreed black people would be enslaved, it was sexism that determined that the lot of the black female would be harsher, more brutal than that of the black male slave. That sexism was not limited solely to white men. The slaveowner's encouragement of mating between black women and men led to the establishment of a black slave sub-culture. Within the black slave sub-culture a similar sexual politics emerged. Initially, slave women were compelled by their masters to mate indiscriminately. It was not uncommon for a master to grant a favored black male slave the privilege of marrying a slave girl or woman of his choice, even if she was a reluctant partner. This practice was not successful. Resistance to forced mating often led to such social upheavals that most masters deemed it wiser to allow black slave women and men to choose their own partners. The couple would make others aware of their commitment by setting up a nuclear household in a vacant hut or cabin. As the displaced Africans assimilated American values, they wanted to have the ecclesiastical and civil ceremonies their masters and mistresses had; they desired public acknowledgement of their union. Although there were never any legally acknowledged marriages between slaves, they wanted the same marriage rituals their white owners enacted. On some plantations slaves carried out traditional African marriage rites—the asking of relatives for a woman's hand and the offering of a small dowry. Many white plantation owners incorporated the practice of engaged couples holding hands and jumping over a broom as a marriage ritual for slaves as it had once been a popular ritual among early American white colonizers. On a few plantations, masters allowed marriage ceremonies to be performed by an ordained minister despite the fact that the service had no legal significance. Most slaves desired a minister to perform the marriage ceremony because they observed that this was a norm of the dominant culture. Undoubtedly courtships and marriages between slaves were important because the happiness of such occasions augmented the harsh reality of slave life. In his slave narrative, Thomas Jones declared that the slave who was:

despised and trampled upon by a cruel race of unfeeling men would die in the prime of his wretched life, if he found no refuge in a dear home, where love and sympathy shall meet him from hearts made sacred to him by his own irrepressible affections and tendernesses for them.

Sex roles in the black slave sub-culture mirrored those of patriarchal white America. Within the black slave sub-culture, it was the black female who cooked for the family, cleaned the hut or cabin, nursed the sick, washed and mended the clothes, and cared for the needs of children. Black slave men regarded tasks like cooking, sewing, nursing, and even minor farm labor as woman's work. In her study of white women in the south, *The Southern Lady*, Anne Scott describes an incident in which a black slave man refused to perform a task he considered beneath his male dignity:

> On a farm in a moment of crisis when the mother and all the children were ill, a Negro slave rejected in bewilderment the suggestion, that he milk the cow, on the grounds that everybody knew that to be woman's work and therefore impossible for him to undertake.

While enslaved black men were in no position to be completely accepted as patriarchal authority figures with the right to rule over women, enslaved black females did conform to existing sex-role patterns that granted men higher status than women. Frances Butler Leigh (the daughter of Fanny Kemble) noted that among slaves in the Georgia Sea Islands "the good old law of female submission to the husband's will on all points held good." Acceptance of male superiority was particularly emphasized in the religious teachings preached to slaves. Christian slave women resolutely believed that it was natural that they be subservient to men. A plantation owner from Lounders Count, Mississippi, Mr. William Ervin, set up rules to govern his slaves which were based on the sex role patterns established by patriarchy. One rule read:

> Each family to live in their own house. The husbands to provide fire wood and see that they are all provided for and wait on his wife. The wife to cook and wash for the husband and her children and attend to the mending of clothes. Failure on either part when proven shall and must be

corrected by words first but if not reformed to be corrected by the whip.

The practice of masters and mistresses identifying a slave woman by her husband's name (Scipio's Jane or John's Sue), indicates that whites accorded the black male slave a higher status than that of the female slave. Historian Eugene Genovese contends:

> Sensible masters actually encouraged a limited sexual division of labor among their slaves and saw some advantages in strengthening the power of the male in the household.

As regards hierarchies based solely on race, the social status of black women and men was the same, but sexist differentiation caused the lot of the male to be distinguished from that of the female. A measure of social equality existed between the sexes in the area of work but nowhere else. Black women and men often performed the exact same tasks in agricultural labor, but even in that area black women could not rise to leadership positions. Outside the work arena, in day-to-day life, female slaves were treated differently from male slaves and were in some instances the subordinates of male slaves.

In an attempt to explain the impact of slavery on black sex role patterns, many contemporary scholars have concluded that the black woman was a more important figure in the slave household than the black male, and that as a result masculinity was compromised. An undue emphasis on black "masculinity" has emerged as sociologists and historians have attempted to explain the damaging effects of racist oppression on black people. Misinformation began circulating when scholars shifted the burden of responsibility away from the institution of slavery and its white supporters onto black people. As part of their effort to explain the negative impact of slavery on the black family without placing the blame or responsibility on white racism, they argued that it could be understood in the framework of black male-female sexual politics. They reasoned that as the black female's role in the slave household was more important than that of the black male, his masculinity had been compromised and consequently the fabric of the black family structure dissolved. They identify the culprit as the domineering black woman. White racist colonizers distorted reality when they talked about the de-masculinization of black men. In actuality, there was nothing unusual about slave women assuming a dominant role in the domestic household in 19th century America. In so doing, they were merely imitating the behavior of white mistresses. The dominant role white women played in the 19th century domestic household has not led scholars to theorize about ineffectual white masculinity; quite the opposite has occurred. The 19th century is usually seen as a period in American history when white patriarchy was the stronghold of the American family. But this strong white patriarchy did not prevent 19th century white women from assuming the dominant role in the household. Nancy Cott, author of *Bonds of Womanhood*, describes the discrepancy between the patriarchal ideal that would have had white men be the supreme head of the household and the 19th century reality:

> Legally and economically the husband/father controlled the family, but rhetorically the vocation of domesticity gave women the domestic sphere for their own, to control, and influence. Motherhood was proposed as the central lever with which women would bridge the world and, in practice it offered the best opportunity to women to heighten their domestic power. The authors of "domestic education" books assumed that children lived mostly in the presence of their mothers and not their fathers, even though final authority (legally and conventionally) was patriarchal.

It is safe to assume that if white women playing a dominant role in the 19th century domestic household did not lead to the de-masculinization and undermining of white male power, the enslaved black woman playing a dominant role in the slave household represented no threat to the already powerless black male. The major distinction between the familial role played by white male slaveowners and that of black male slaves within the sub-culture was that black men were denied the opportunity to act as providers for their families. According to some scholars, it was the inability of black men to adequately provide coupled with the dominant role played by black women in slave households that resulted in de-masculinization. They ignore two realities. First, that in 19th century America emphasis on the home and family as "woman's sphere" was all pervasive, so that it was not unusual for the role played by black women to take precedence over that of black men. And the reality was that black men were able workers and providers, only white people reaped the benefits of their labor. It is ludicrous to assume that black men who labored at their various tasks from twelve to sixteen hours a day had doubts about their ability to provide— and is probably more accurate to assert that enslaved black men, rather than feeling de-masculinized, were outraged and angry that racist oppression prevented them from reaping the benefits of their labor. In keeping with the sexual politics of 19th century America, many black slave men felt very strongly that it was their duty to provide for the economic well-being of their family and they felt bitter resentment and remorse that the slave system did not enable them to fulfill this role. Feeling remorse, anger, and resentment cannot be seen as synonymous with feeling de-masculinized.

Enslaved black people accepted patriarchal definitions of male-female sex roles. They believed, as did their white owners, that woman's role entailed remaining in the domestic household, rearing children, and obeying the will of husbands. Anne Scott sums up the image of the 19th century idealized woman in the following passage:

> This marvelous creation was described as a submissive wife whose reason for being was to love, honor, obey, and occasionally amuse her husband, to bring up his children and manage his household. Physically weak, and 'formed for the less laborious occupations,' she depended upon male protection. To secure this protection she was endowed with the capacity to 'create a magic spell' over any man in her vicinity. She was timid and modest, beautiful and graceful, 'the most fascinating being in creation... the delight and charm of every circle she moves in.'
> Part of her charm lay in her innocence.... She was capable of acute perceptions about human relationships, and was a creature of tact, discernment, sympathy, and compassion. It was her nature to be self-denying, and she was given to suffering in silence, a characteristic said to endear her to men. Less endearing, perhaps, but no less natural, was her piety and her tendency to 'restrain man's

natural vice and immorality.' She was thought to be most deeply interested in the success of every scheme which curbs the passions and enforces a true morality.'

The "cult of true womanhood" that emerged during the 19th century had an intense demoralizing impact on enslaved black females. They were not proud of their ability to labor alongside men in the fields and wanted more than anything for their lot to be the same as that of white women. White male slaveowners and overseers found that slave women could best be manipulated by promises of a new dress, a hair ribbon, or a parasol—anything that emphasized their femininity. So great was the slave woman's desire to appear feminine and ladylike that many chose to wear dresses to work in the fields rather than don trousers that, though more practical, were seen as masculine attire. Originally displaced African women attached no stigma to female labor in the fields but as they assimilated white American values they accepted the notion that it was debasing and degrading for women to work in the fields. As a farm laborer, the black male slave performed the same tasks he would have had to perform as a free person, but black women were well aware that it was not deemed ladylike or respectable for women to work in the fields. Henry Watson, a plantation owner in Alabama, complained to his daughter in 1865 about the black female workers on his plantation:

> The women say that they never mean to do anymore outdoor work, that white men support their wives; and they mean that their husbands shall support them.

Although black female slaves often boasted of their work ability, they longed to be treated with the same regard and consideration they believed was due them as a woman's privilege in patriarchal society. Watson reported at a later date:

> The female laborers are almost invariably idle—do not go into the fields but desire to play the lady and be supported by their husbands 'like the white folks do.'

The fact that enslaved black women were forced to labor as "men" and to exist independently of male protection and provision did not lead to the development of a feminist consciousness. They did not advocate social equality between the sexes. Instead they bitterly resented that they were not considered "women" by the dominant culture and therefore were not the recipients of the considerations and privileges given white women. Modesty, sexual purity, innocence, and a submissive manner were the qualities associated with womanhood and femininity that enslaved black women endeavored to attain even though the conditions under which they lived continually undermined their efforts. When freedom came, black women resolved to cease their labor in the fields. White plantation owners were shocked when large numbers of black female workers refused to work in the fields once slavery ended. An examination of 1865 and 1866 plantation records caused Theodore Wilson to surmise that "the greatest loss to the labor force resulted from the decision of growing numbers of Negro women to donate their time to their homes and children." On those plantations where black women continued to labor in the fields, owners complained that they left their cabins too late in the morning and quit too early in the afternoon. White Southerners expressed amazement that it was a matter of pride among black people for men to support their wives and families. In some cases whites so resented the loss of female workers that they charged black men extra for food and shelter if their wives did not work. By completely accepting the female role as defined by patriarchy, enslaved black women embraced and upheld an oppressive sexist social order and became (along with their white sisters) both accomplices in the crimes perpetrated against women and the victims of those crimes.

2

Continued Devaluation
of Black Womanhood

Scholars who write about mass sexual exploitation of black women during slavery rarely discuss its political and social impact on the status of black women. In her important feminist analysis of rape, *Against Our Will*, Susan Brownmiller neglects this issue in the section on slavery. She comments:

> Rape in slavery was more than a chance tool of violence. It was an institutionalized crime, part and parcel of the white man's subjugation of a people for economic and psychological gain.

Brownmiller seemingly acknowledges the importance of discussing the rape of black women during slavery by including such a section in her book, she effectively dismisses it by emphasizing that this was history, past, over with. Her chapter is titled, "Two Studies in American Experience." And she begins with the statement:

> The American experience of the slave South, which spanned two centuries, is a perfect study of rape in all its complexities for the black woman's sexual integrity was deliberately crushed in order that slavery might profitably endure.

While Brownmiller successfully impresses upon readers the fact that white men brutally assaulted black women during slavery, she minimizes the impact that oppression has had on all black women in America by placing it solely in the limited historical context of an "institutionalized crime" during slavery. In so doing she fails to see that the significance of the rape of enslaved black women was not simply that it "deliberately crushed" their sexual integrity for economic ends but that it led to a devaluation of black womanhood that permeated the psyches of all Americans and shaped the social status of all black women once slavery ended. One has only to look at American television twenty-four hours a day for an entire week to learn the way in which black women are perceived in American society—the predominant image is that of the "fallen" woman, the whore, the slut, the prostitute.

The success of sexist-racist conditioning of American people to regard black women as creatures of little worth or value is evident when politically conscious white feminists minimize sexist oppression of black women, as Brownmiller does. She does not inform readers that white men continued to sexually assault black women long after slavery ended and that such rapes were socially sanctioned. She does not make the point that a primary reason rape of black women has never received what little attention rape of white women receives is because black women have always been seen by the white public as sexually permissive, as available and eager for the sexual assaults of any man, black or white. The designation of all black women as sexually depraved, immoral, and loose had its roots in the slave system. White women and men justified the sexual exploitation of enslaved black women by arguing that they were the initiators of sexual relationships with men. From such thinking emerged the stereotype of black women as sexual savages, and in sexist terms a sexual savage, a non-human, an animal cannot be raped. It is difficult to believe that Brownmiller is ignorant of these realities; I can only assume she deems them unimportant.

As far back as slavery, white people established a social hierarchy based on race and sex that ranked white men first, white women second, though sometimes equal to black men, who are ranked third, and black women last. What this means in terms of the sexual politics of rape is that if one white woman is raped by a black man, it is seen as more important, more significant than if thousands of black women are raped by one white man. Most Americans, and that includes black people, acknowledge and accept this hierarchy; they have internalized it either consciously or unconsciously. And for this reason, all through American history, black male rape of white women has attracted much more attention and is seen as much more significant than rape of black women by either white or black men. Brownmiller further perpetuates the belief that the real danger to women of interracial sexual exploitation in American society is black male rape of white females. One of the longest chapters in her book is on this subject. It is significant that she titles her discussion of the rape of Native American women and black women by white men "a Study in American History" but titles her section of black male rape of white women "A Question of Race." In the opening paragraph to this section she writes, "Racism and sexism and the fight against both converge at the point of interracial rape, the baffling crossroads of an authentic, peculiarly American dilemma." Brownmiller fails to mention terms like "interracial rape" or "sexism" in her chapters dealing with the rape of non-white women.

A devaluation of black womanhood occurred as a result of the sexual exploitation of black women during slavery that has not altered in the course of hundreds of years. I have previously mentioned that while many concerned citizens sympathized with the sexual exploitation of black women both during slavery and afterwards, like all rape victims in patriarchal society they were seen as having lost value and worth as a result of the humiliation they endured. Annals of slavery reveal that the same abolitionist public that condemned the rape of black women regarded them as accomplices rather than victims. In her diary, the southern white woman Mary Boykin Chesnut recorded:

(March 14, 1861.) Under slavery, we live surrounded by

prostitutes, yet an abandoned woman is sent out of any decent house. Who thinks any worse of a Negro or mulatto woman for being a thing we can't name? God, forgive us, but ours is a monstrous system, a wrong and an inequity! Like the patriarchs of old, our men live all in one house with their wives and their concubines; and the mulattoes one sees in every family partly resemble the white children. Any lady is ready to tell you who is the father of all the mulatto children in everybody's household but her own. Those, she seems to think, drop from the clouds. My disgust sometimes is boiling over. Thank God for my country women, but alas for the men! They are probably no worse than men everywhere, but the lower the mistress, the more degraded they must be.

(April 20, 1861.) Bad books are not allowed house room except in the library under lock and key, the key is in the Master's pocket; but bad women, if they are not white and serve in a menial capacity, may swarm the house unmolested. The ostrich game is thought a Christian act. These women are no more regarded as a dangerous contingent than canary birds would be.

(Aug. 22, 1861.) I hate slavery. You say there are no more fallen women on a plantation than in London, in proportion to numbers; but what do you say to this? A magnate who runs a hideous black harem with its consequences under the same roof with his lovely white wife and his beautiful and accomplished daughters?

These diary entries indicate that Chesnut held enslaved black women responsible for their fate. Her wrath and anger is aimed at them and not at white men. Although stereotypical images of black womanhood during slavery were based on the myth that all black women were immoral and sexually loose, slave narratives and diaries of the 19th century present no evidence that they were in any way more sexually "liberated" than white women. The great majority of enslaved black women accepted the dominant culture's sexual morality and adapted it to their circumstances. Black slave girls were taught, like their white counterparts, that virtue was woman's ideal spiritual nature and virginity her ideal physical state, but knowledge of the acceptable sexual morality did not alter the reality that no social order existed to protect them from sexual exploitation.

When slavery ended, black women and men welcomed their newly acquired freedom to express their sexuality. Like the early white colonizers, newly manumitted black folks were without any social order to govern and restrain their sexual behavior and indulged themselves with proper abandon. It must have been a good feeling for the manumitted slaves to suddenly have the freedom to choose a sexual partner and to behave in whatever manner they so desired. Some manumitted black women exercised their new found sexual freedom by engaging freely in sexual relationships with black men. Whites saw the sexual activity of the manumitted female slave as further evidence to support their claim that black women were sexually loose and innately morally depraved. They chose to ignore the fact that the great majority of black women and men attempted to adapt the values and behavior patterns deemed acceptable by whites. During the years of Black Reconstruction, 1867-77, black women struggled to change negative images of black womanhood perpetuated by whites. Trying to dispel the myth that all black women were sexually loose, they emulated the conduct and mannerisms of white women. But as manumitted black women and men struggled to change stereotypical images of black female sexuality, white society resisted. Everywhere black women went, on public streets, in shops, or at their places of work, they were accosted and subjected to obscene comments and even physical abuse at the hands of white men and women. Those black women suffered most whose behavior best exemplified that of a "lady". A black woman dressed tidy and clean, carrying herself in a dignified manner, was usually the object of mud-slinging by white men who ridiculed and mocked her self-improvement efforts. They reminded her that in the eyes of the white public she would never be seen as worthy of consideration or respect.

White journalists daily ridiculed the efforts of black people to improve their image in leading magazines and newspapers. They delighted in entertaining white readers with negative stereotypes of black people. Rayford Logan examines the extent to which leading newspapers and magazines deliberately perpetuated negative myths and stereotypes about black people in his study of the period from 1877 to 1918, *The Betrayal of the*

Negro. Logan acknowledges that whites made a concerted effort to perpetuate the myth that all black women were sexually loose and immoral. He comments:

> The alleged unchastity of Negro women in general was analyzed in an article in the *Atlantic*. The practice was attributed to their lack of concern for sexual purity and to the free use that white men made of them. The author added that the sexual immorality of Negro women was a deterrent to loose morals between white men and white women.

Articles of this type were aimed at maintaining separation of the races. They convinced white readers that they would not want to live as social equals with black people by arguing that contact with the loose morals of blacks (and particularly those of black women) would lead to a breakdown of all moral values. The white public justified white male sexual assault of black females by arguing that the women invited sexual abuse by their lack of morals.

Sexual exploitation of black women undermined the morale of newly manumitted black people. For it seemed to them that if they could not change negative images of black womanhood they would never be able to uplift the race as a whole. Married or single, child or woman, the black female was a likely target for white male rapists. Young black girls were admonished by concerned parents to avoid walking down isolated streets and to avoid contact with white men whenever possible. While these practices curtailed sexual exploitation, it was not eliminated because most sexual assaults occurred on jobs. A young, newly married black woman employed as cook for a white female reported that only a short period of time lapsed before she was accosted by the white husband:

> I remember very well the first and last work place from which I was dismissed. I lost my place because I refused to let the madam's husband kiss me. He must have been accustomed to undue familiarity with his servants, or else he took it as a matter of course, because without any lovemaking at all, soon after I was installed as a cook, he walked up to me, threw his arms around me, and was in the act of kissing me, when I demanded to know what he

meant, and shoved him away. I was young then, and newly married, and didn't know then what has been a burden to my mind and heart ever since, that a colored woman's virtue in this part of the country has no protection. I at once went home, and told my husband about it. When my husband went to the man who had insulted me, the man cursed him, and slapped him, and—had him arrested! The police judge fined my husband $25. I was present at the hearing and testified on oath to the insult offered me. The white man, of course, denied the charge. The old judge looked up and said, "This court will never take the word of a nigger against the word of a white man."

Black women were often coerced into sexual liaisons with white employers who would threaten to fire them unless they capitulated to sexual demands. One black woman stated:

I believe nearly all white men take, and expect to take undue liberties with their colored female servants—not only the father, but in many cases the sons also. Those servants who rebel against such familiarity must either leave or expect a mighty hard time, if they stay. By comparison those who tamely admit to these improper relations live in clover. They always have a little spending change, wear better clothes, and are able to get off from work at least once a week—and sometimes oftener. This moral debasement is not at all times unknown to the white women in these homes. I know of more than one colored woman who was openly importuned by white women to become the mistresses of their white husbands, on the grounds that they, the white wives, were afraid that, if their husbands did not associate with colored women, they would certainly do so with outside white women, and the white wives, for reasons which ought to be perfectly obvious, preferred to have their husbands do wrong with the colored women in order to keep their husbands straight.

The sexual assault of black women was so prevalent in both the North and the South after slavery ended that outraged black women and men wrote articles in newspapers and magazines pleading with the American public to take action against white and black male offenders who assaulted black women. An article published in the January 1912 issue of the *Independent* written by a black nurse pleaded for an end to sexual abuse:

> We poor colored women wage-earners in the South are
> fighting a terrible battle.... On the one hand, we are assailed
> by white men, and, on the other hand, we are assailed by
> black men, who should be our natural protectors; and
> whether in the cook kitchen, at the washtub, over the
> sewing machine, behind the baby carriage, or at the ironing
> board, we are but little more than pack horses, beasts of
> burden, slaves! In the distant future, it may be, centuries
> and centuries hence, a monument of brass or stone will be
> erected to the Old Black Mammies of the South, but what
> we need is present help, present sympathy, better wages,
> better hours, more protection, and a chance to breathe for
> once while alive as free women.

When black people urged the white public to aid them in their
struggles to protect black womanhood, their appeals fell on
deaf ears. So pervasive was the tendency of whites to regard all
black women as sexually loose and unworthy of respect that
their achievements were ignored. Even if an individual black
female became a lawyer, doctor, or teacher, she was likely to be
labeled a whore or prostitute by whites. All black women,
irrespective of their circumstances, were lumped into the category of available sex objects. As late as the 60s, black woman
playwright Lorraine Hansberry in *To Be Young, Gifted, and
Black* included scenes that dramatized the way in which all
black women are perceived by whites (and in particular white
men), as available sex objects, as prostitutes. In the play a young
black domestic worker says:

> All right. So now you know something 'bout me you didn't
> know! In these streets out there, any little white boy from
> Long Island or Westchester sees me and leans out of his car
> and yells—"Hey there, hot choclate! Say there Jezebel! Hey
> you—'Hundred Dollar Misunderstanding! YOU! Bet you
> know where there's a good time tonight...."
>   Follow me sometimes and see if I lie. I can be coming
> home from eight hours on an assembly line or fourteen
> hours in Mrs. Halsey's kitchen. I can be all filled up that day
> with three hundred years of rage so that my eyes are
> flashing and my flesh is trembling—and the white boys in
> the streets, they look at me and think of sex. They look at
> me and that's all they think... Baby, you could be Jesus in
> drag—but if you're brown they're sure you're selling!

Hansberry shows that this attitude toward black women transcended class boundaries. Later in the play a chic black professional woman of middle-age speaks:

> 'Hey there, hot chocolate! Say there, Jezebel! YOU...! The white boys in the streets, they look at me and think of sex. They look at me and that's all they think!

Like Susan Brownmiller, most people tend to see devaluation of black womanhood as occurring only in the context of slavery. In actuality, sexual exploitation of black women continued long after slavery ended and was institutionalized by other oppressive practices. Devaluation of black womanhood after slavery ended was a conscious, deliberate effort on the part of whites to sabotage mounting black female self-confidence and self-respect. In *Black Women in White America*, Gerda Lerner discusses the "complex system of supportive mechanisms and sustaining myths" white women and men established to encourage sexual exploitation of black women and to ensure no change would occur in their social status:

> One of these was the myth of the "bad" black woman. By assuming a different level of sexuality for all Blacks than that of whites and mythifying their greater sexual potency, the black woman could be made to personify sexual freedom and abandon. A myth was created that all black women were eager for sexual exploits, voluntarily "loose" in their morals and, therefore deserved none of the consideration and respect granted white women. Every black woman was, by definition, a slut according to this racist mythology; therefore, to assault her and exploit her sexually was not reprehensible and carried with it none of the normal communal sanctions against such behavior. A wide range of practices reinforced this myth: the laws against intermarriage; the denial of the title "Miss" or "Mrs." to any black woman; the taboos against respectable social mixing of the races; the refusal to let black women customers try on clothing in stores before making a purchase; the assigning of single toilet facilities to both sexes of Blacks; the different legal sanction against rape, abuse of minors and other sex crimes when committed against white or black women.

Systematic devaluation of black womanhood was not simply a

direct consequence of race hatred, it was a calculated method of social control. During the reconstruction years, manumitted black people had demonstrated that given the same opportunities as whites they could excel in all areas. Their accomplishments were a direct challenge to racist notions about the inherent inferiority of dark races. In those glorious years, it seemed that black people would quickly and successfully assimilate and amalgamate into the mainstream of American culture. White people reacted to the progress of black people by attempting to return to the old social order. To maintain white supremacy they established a new social order based on apartheid. The period in American history is commonly known as the Jim Crow or "separate but equal" years, but both phrases shift attention away from the fact that separation of the races once slavery ended was a deliberate political move on the part of white supremacists. As miscegenation represented the greatest threat to white racial solidarity, a complex system of laws and social taboos was enacted to maintain separation of the races. In most states laws were enacted forbidding inter-racial marriage, but such laws did not prevent blacks and whites from uniting. Manumitted black men and white women in northern states were married in noticeable numbers. White men, who so desired, legalized relationships with ex-slave women. A report of a marriage between a white man and a black woman published in a New Orleans newspaper, the *Tribune*, carried the headlines, "The World Moves." In the article, the journalist advised other white men to "take a hint now that the law allows it legitimize their children." Inter-racial marriages between black women and white men evoked fear and rage in the white public. White male legalized sexual unions with black women and black male legalized sexual unions with white women threatened the entire foundation of apartheid. Since anti-amalgamation laws were not sufficient deterrents to inter-racial marriage, white men used psychological warfare to enforce the ideal of white supremacy. They employed two important myths to brainwash all whites against the newly manumitted blacks: the myth of the "bad," sexually loose black woman and the myth of the black male rapist. Neither myth was based on fact.

At no time in the early part of the 20th century were any large numbers of black men raping white women or seeking illicit relationships with them. Joseph Washington, Jr.'s, study of inter-racial union, *Marriage in Black and White*, documents the fact that black men who sought relationships with white women were eager for marriage. White people were never reacting to any high incidence of inter-racial rape during reconstruction; they simply wanted to prevent inter-racial marriage. They used lynchings, castration, and other brutal punishments to prevent black men from initiating relationships with white women. They perpetuated the myth that all black men were eager to rape white women so that white females would not seek friendships with black men for fear of brutal assault. The horrific nature of violent attacks on black manhood has caused historiographers and sociologists to assume that whites feared unions between white women and black men most. In actuality, they feared legally sanctioned racial mixing on the part of the sexes of either group, but as black men were more likely to seek legal sanction through marriage of their relationships with white women, they received the brunt of attacks by white supremacists. By brainwashing white women to see black men as savage beasts, white supremacists were able to implant enough fear in the white female's psyche so that she would avoid any contact with black men.

In the case of black women and white men, inter-racial sex was both encouraged and condoned as long as it did not lead to marriage. By perpetuating the myth that all black women were incapable of fidelity and sexually loose, whites hoped to so devalue them that no white man would marry a black woman. After manumission, white men who treated black women with respect or sought to integrate a black female into respectable white society were persecuted and ostracized. During slavery, it had been a common occurrence for an upper class or middle class white man to take a black woman mistress and live openly with her without incurring much public disapproval. In *Roll, Jordan, Roll* Eugene Genovese comments:

> Some prominent planters flaunted their slave mistresses

and mulatto children. David Dickson of Georgia, one of the most celebrated leaders in the movement to reform southern agriculture, lost his wife early in life, took a mistress, and accepted a measure of social disapproval to live openly with her and their children. Bennett H. Barrow of Louisiana exploded with rage over similar conduct on the part of his neighbors. His fellow planters of West Feliciana Parish were, he said, of course all opponents of the abolitionists. "Yet, the people submit to amalgamation in its worst form in this Parish. Josias Grey takes his mulatto children with him to public places, etc. and receives similar company from New Orleans..." The first mayor of Memphis, Marcus Winchester, had a beautiful quadroon mistress whom he married and took to Louisiana. His successor, Ike Rawlins, lived with a slave woman. He did not marry her but did provide handsomely for their sons. And the haughty nabobs of Natches had their own scandals. Other white observers report such relationships, displayed publicly and accepted by society with nothing worse than muttering and minor social ostracism. Several daughters of wealthy free Negroes married respectable white men.

Marriages between black women and white men could be tolerated during slavery because they were so few in number and represented no threat to the white supremacist regime. After manumission they were no longer tolerated. In the state of Kentucky, the Supreme Court was asked to judge insane a white man who desired to marry a female slave he had once owned. Once slavery ended and whites declared that no black woman regardless of her class status or skin color could ever be a "lady," it was no longer socially acceptable for a white man to have a black mistress. Instead, the institutionalized devaluation of black womanhood encouraged all white men to regard black females as whores or prostitutes. Lower class white men, who had had little sexual contact with black women during slavery, were encouraged to believe they were entitled to access to the bodies of black women. In large cities their lust for black female sex objects led to the formation of numerous houses of prostitution which supplied black bodies to meet the growing demands of white men. The myth perpetuated by whites that black women were the possessors of a heightened sexuality encouraged white male rapists and sexual exploiters. This myth so dominated the psyches of whites that a southern white male writer asserts:

> I knew all about the sexual act, but not until I was twelve years old did I know that it was performed with white women for pleasure; I had thought that only Negro women engaged in the act of love with white men just for fun, because they were the only ones with the animal desire to submit that way.

Racial integration in the latter part of the 20th century caused many barriers against inter-racial marriages to be torn down. Yet the amalgamation of the races that sociologists had predicted might take place did not occur. While black men married white women in ever-increasing numbers, large numbers of white men did not marry black women. These differences in responses were no accident. While changes in public attitudes toward black men had occurred, there had not been any change in negative images of black women. The myth that all black men were rapists had ceased to dominate the consciousness of the American public by the 70s. One explanation for the change was the growing knowledge of the way in which this myth was used by whites in power to persecute and torture black men. Once the myth was no longer accepted as absolute truth, white women who so desired could freely engage in relationships with black men and vice versa.

The success of movies like *Guess Who's Coming to Dinner* and *The Great White Hope* revealed that the white American public was not averse to acknowledging attractions between black men and white women that led to marriage. The public's acceptance of these movies indicates that it no longer feared black males and white females uniting. While the myth that all black men are rapists is no longer perpetuated by a majority of whites, they continue to promote the myth that all black women are sexually loose and they use devaluation of black womanhood as a way to discourage marriage between large numbers of white men and black women. White Americans have legally relinquished the apartheid structure that once characterized race relations but they have not given up white rule. Given that power in capitalist patriarchal America is in the hands of white men, the present obvious threat to white solidarity is inter-marriage between white men and non-white women, and in particular black women. As whites have been much more voyeuristically, phobically interested in sexual relationships between white women and black men, the existence of rigid social taboos prohibiting white male marriage to black females is often totally ignored, yet such taboos may prove to have far greater impact on our society than taboos against black male-white female mating. The white American public that could dismiss with disinterest contemporary showings of movies like *Guess Who's Coming to Dinner* that depict black male marriage to a white woman on national television reacted with outrage and anger when a day time soap opera, *Days of Our Lives*, aired a program in which a respectable young white male was shown falling in love with a black female.

Taboos against white women mating with black men were maintained by white men because they were interested in limiting the sexual freedom of white women and insuring that their female "property" was not trespassed on by black men. Now that improved male-invented contraceptive devices have diminished the emphasis on female sexual purity and provided all men greater access to women's bodies, white men have shown less interest in overseeing the sexual activities of white women. In contemporary times, marriages between black men and white women are more readily accepted and occur in ever increasing numbers. Explanations as to why marriages between white women and black men are more readily accepted than marriages between white men and black women can be found in patriarchal sexual politics. Since white women represent a powerless group when not allied with powerful white men, their marriage to black men is no great threat to existing white patriarchal rule. In our patriarchal society if a wealthy white woman marries a black man she legally adopts his status. Accordingly a black woman who marries a white man adopts his status; she takes his name and their children are his heirs. Consequently, if a large majority of that small group of white men who dominate decision-making bodies in American society were to marry black women, the foundation of white rule would be threatened.

A complex system of negative myths and stereotypes daily socializes white men to regard black women as unsuitable marriage partners. In American history, white men have never sought to marry black women in as great numbers as black men have sought to marry white women. Scholars have argued that since white men have always had "free," unlimited access to the bodies of black women they have seen no need to legitimize these relationships by marriage. This argument fails to show consideration of the various factors that determine marriage suitability. Joseph Washington comments:

> White men have failed to be serious in their relationships with the black woman in comparison to the seriousness of relationships between the black man and the white woman.

He offers as an explanation for this attitude white male perception of black women as "beasts," sexual savages who are unfit for marriage. Washington does not discuss the fact that white people deliberately perpetuate myths about black female bestial sexuality so as to discourage white men from seeing black women as suitable marriage partners. Whites condone inter-racial relationships between black women and white men only in the context of degrading sex. The mass media, especially television, is one way that negative images of black womanhood continue to be impressed upon all our psyches. In the daytime soap opera in which the young white man falls in love with a black female, she is depicted solely in terms of negative stereotypes. Her features are distorted by excessive make-up, a greasy type substance is used on her lips in order to make them look thicker than they are; she wears a wig and dresses in garments that cause her to seem slightly overweight. In real life the black woman in no way resembles the character she portrays on the soap, and she is the only character who is made to look radically different, whose features are grossly distorted. Without the distortions she is a healthy, attractive looking woman who in no way resembles white people's negative stereotype of black women. Significantly, the facial features of the white woman who is her rival are not altered in any way. In recent years, the most revolting image of black womanhood on television was portrayed in a situation comedy called *Detective School.* There the black woman is constantly ridiculed for her ugliness, her bad temper, etc. White men in the show are either mocking her or attacking her physically. The white women she is contrasted with are blonde and stereotypically attractive. In other television shows the predominant image of black women is that of the sex object, prostitute, and whore, etc. The second image is that of the overweight nagging maternal figure. Even those shows that have cast black female children depict them within the framework of negative stereotypes. The little black girl on the situation comedy *What's Happening* was portrayed as a miniature Sapphire—constantly nagging and telling tales on her brother. Black women have fared no better in American film. A recent film with another image of black womanhood was *Remember My Name*, a movie that was glorifying the toughness of today's "liberated" white woman. Significantly, a measure of her toughness is that she is able to beat and brutalize a black woman who just happens to have a white boyfriend. The images of black women that are seen as positive usually are those that depict the black woman as a longsuffering, religious, maternal figure, whose most endearing characteristic is her self-sacrificing self-denial for those she loves.

Negative images of black women in television and film are not simply impressed upon the psyches of white males, they affect all Americans. Black mothers and fathers constantly complain that television lowers the self-confidence and self-esteem of black girls. Even on television commercials the black female child is rarely visible—largely because sexist-racist Americans tend to see the black male as the representative of the black race. So commercials and advertisements in magazines may portray a white female and male but feel that it is enough to have a black male to represent black people. The same logic occurs in regular television programs. On many shows there are single black male figures or single black female figures but rarely are a black woman and man together. In some instances as is often the case on *Saturday Night Live*, black men dress in female clothing and portray black women, usually mocking and ridiculing them. Whites who control media exclude black women so as to emphasize their undesirability either as friends or sexual partners. This also promotes divisiveness between black men and black women, for white people are saying via their manipulation of black roles that they accept black men but not black women. And black women are not accepted because they are seen as a threat to the existing race-sex hierarchy.

While negative images of black womanhood are used to impress upon white men their undesirability as marriage partners, the belief that all white men desire from black women is illicit sex prevents black women from seeking such unions. Just as whites have not been interested in myths and stereotypes black people perpetuate about them, there is little discussion of the fact that the idea that all white men are eager to rape black women continues to be a widespread belief in black communities. Of course this belief was once based on the actual fact that for many years large numbers of white men could and did sexually exploit black women. The fact that this may no longer be the case has not caused black people (and in particular black men) to change their attitudes, largely because many black people are just as committed to racial solidarity as white people and they believe it can best be maintained by discouraging legalized union between white men and black women.

Black men have a vested interest in maintaining existing barriers which discourage black female-white male marriage, for it eliminates sexual competition. Just as sexist white folks used the idea that all black men were rapists to limit the sexual freedom of white women, black people employ the same tactic to control black female sexual behavior. For many years, black people warned black females to beware involvement with white men for fear such relationships would lead to exploitation and degradation of black womanhood. While there is no need to deny the historical fact that white men have sexually exploited black women, this knowledge is used by the white and black public as a psychological weapon to limit and restrain the freedom of black females. Black females who have been socialized by parents to feel threatened or even terrorized by contact with white men often have difficulty relating to white male employers, teachers, doctors, etc. There are many black women who have as phobic a fear about white male sexuality as the fear white women have traditionally felt towards black men. Phobic fear is not a solution to the problem of sexual exploitation or rape. It is a symptom. While an awareness of male power to rape women with impunity in a patriarchal society is necessary for woman's survival, it is even more important that women realize that they can prevent such assaults and protect themselves should they occur.

In a class on Black Women I taught at the University of Southern California, black female students discussed their fear of white men and their anger and rage that white men approached them at jobs, in restaurants, hallways, or on elevators and made sexual overtures. Most women in the class agreed that to avoid these negative encounters they are never friendly with white men, ignore them, or send hostile vibrations in their direction. They also acknowledged that many aggressive sexual overtures by white men, seen as insulting and negative, were casually dismissed or even seen as positive when made by black men. Since they perceived white male sexual overtures as racist, they could not understand that the sexism motivating these acts was not that different from the sexism motivating aggressive sexual overtures of black men.

The emphasis on the white male as sexual exploiter in black communities often deflects attention away from black male sexual exploitation of black women. Many black parents who warned their daughters against the sexual overtures of white men did not warn them about black male exploiters. Since black men were seen as possible marriage candidates, it was more acceptable for them to cajole and seduce black women into potentially sexually exploitative relationships. While black parents admonished daughters not to submit to sexual assaults by white men, they were not encouraging them to reject similar approaches from black men. This is just another indication of the way in which the pervasive concern black people have about racism allows them to conveniently ignore the reality of sexist oppression. They have not been willing to acknowledge that while racism caused white men to make black women targets, it was and is sexism that causes all men to think that they can verbally or physically assault women sexually with impunity. In the final analysis, in the case of white male sexual exploitation of black women, it is the sexism motivating these assaults that is important and not just the racial background of the men who initiate them. It was common during the sixties' black power movement for black men to overemphasize white male sexual exploitation of black womanhood as a way to explain their disapproval of inter-racial relationships involving the two groups. Often they were merely interested in controlling black females sexually. While self-proclaimed black nationalist male leaders felt that it was no contradiction of their political views to have white women companions (after all they were only exercising their right as "men" in a patriarchal society to do as they please in their private life) they were horrified, outraged, and angry with black women who accepted white male companions. There has yet to be a prominent black female political activist who has shown a marked preference for white male companions and if there were, such a relationship would not be at all acceptable to black people.

White males who desire friendships or marriage with black females often find their friendly overture rebuffed or dismissed by the woman in question. Male scholars, black and white, who have written about inter-racial marriage practices (*Marriage in Black and White, Sexual Racism, Sex and Racism in America*) fail to mention that more marriages do not take place between white men and black women because of the reluctance of black females. Black women who date or marry white men find that they cannot endure the harassment and persecution by black and white people. In some instances black men who are themselves involved in inter-racial relationships act contemptuously towards black women who exercise the same freedom of choice. They see their own behavior as acceptable because they view white women as victims, while they see white men as oppressors. So in their eyes a black woman involved with a white man is allying herself with a racist oppressor. But their tendency to see white women as innocent, as non-racist is yet another reflection of their acceptance of sexist idealization of woman. For white women have historically shown themselves to be as capable of being racist oppressors as white men. Another tactic many black men employ to explain their acceptance of inter-racial relationships with white women and their condemnation of black female-white male relations is to assert that they are exploiting white women like white men exploited black women. They evoke a false sense of avenging themselves against racism to mask their sexist exploitative feelings about white women and finally all women. The collective effort on the part of white and black people to curtail marriage and even friendship between black women and white men serves to help maintain white patriarchal rule and to support continued devaluation of black womanhood.

Systematic devaluation of black womanhood led to a downgrading of any activity black women did. Many black women attempted to shift the focus of attention away from sexuality by emphasizing their commitment to motherhood. As participants in the "cult of true womanhood" that reached its peak in early 20th century America, they endeavored to prove their value and worth by demonstrating that they were women whose lives were firmly rooted in the family. They worked diligently in service jobs to provide economically for their children, and demonstrated their love by incredible self-sacrifice. While their efforts were acknowledged by the American public, whites deliberately cast them in a negative light. They labeled hard-working, self-sacrificing black women who were concerned with creating a loving, supportive environment for their families Aunt Jemimas, Sapphires, Amazons—all negative images that were based upon existing sexist stereotypes of womanhood. In more recent years the labeling of black women matriarchs emerged as yet another attempt by the white male power structure to cast the positive contributions of black women in a negative light. All the negative stereotypes used to characterize black women were anti-woman. As sexist ideology has been accepted by black people, these negative myths and stereotypes have effectively transcended class and race boundaries and affected the way black women were perceived by members of their own race and the way they perceived themselves.

Many of the anti-black-woman stereotypes originated during slavery. Long before sociologists perpetuated theories about the existence of a black matriarchy, white male slave-owners created a body of myths to discredit the contributions of black females; one such myth was the notion that they were all masculinized sub-human creatures. Black female slaves had shown that they were capable of performing so-called "manly" labor, that they were able to endure hardship, pain, and privation but could also perform those so-called "womanly" tasks of housekeeping, cooking, and child rearing. Their ability to cope effectively in a sexist-defined "male" role threatened patriarchal myths about the nature of woman's inherent physiological difference and inferiority. By forcing black female slaves to perform the same work tasks as black male slaves, white male patriarchs were contradicting their own sexist order that claimed woman to be inferior because she lacked physical prowess. An explanation had to be provided to explain why black women were able to perform tasks that were cited by patriarchs as jobs women were incapable of performing. To explain the black female's ability to survive without the direct aid of a male and her ability to perform tasks that were culturally defined as "male" work, white males argued that black slave women were not "real" women but were masculinized sub-human creatures. It is not unlikely that white men feared that white women, witnessing the black female slave's ability to cope as effectively in the work force as men, might develop ideas about social equality between the sexes and encourage political solidarity between black and white women. Whatever the reason, black women posed so great a threat to the existing patriarchy that white men perpetuated the notion that black women possessed unusual masculine-like characteristics not common to the female species. To prove their point, they often forced black women to labor at difficult jobs while black male slaves stood idle.

The unwillingness of present-day scholars to accept as a positive step social equality between the sexes in any sphere led to the formation of the theory that a black matriarchy existed in the black family structure. Male social scientists formulated theories about the matriarchal power of black females to provide an out-of-the-ordinary explanation for the independent and decisive role black women played within the black family structure. Like their slaveowning ancestors, racist scholars acted as if black women fulfilling their role as mothers and economic providers were performing a unique action that needed a new definition even though it was not uncommon for many poor and widowed white women to perform this dual role. Yet they labeled black women matriarchs—a title that in no way accurately described the social status of black women in America. No matriarchy has ever existed in the United States.

At the very time sociologists proclaimed the existence of a matriarchal order in the black family structure, black women represented one of the largest socially and economically deprived groups in America whose status in no way resembled that of a matriarch. Political activist Angela Davis writes of the label matriarch:

> The designation of the black woman as a matriarch is a cruel misnomer because it ignores the profound traumas the black woman must have experienced when she had to surrender her child-bearing to alien and predatory economic interest.

The term matriarch implies the existence of a social order in which women exercise social and political power, a state which in no way resembles the condition of black women or all women in American society. The decisions that determine the way in which black women must live their lives are made by others, usually white men. If sociologists are to casually label black women matriarchs, they should also label female children playing house and acting out the role of mother matriarchs. For in both instances, no real effective power exists that allows the females in question to control their own destiny.

In their article "Is the Black Male Castrated," Jean Bond and Pauline Perry write of the matriarchy myth:

> The casting of this image of the black female in sociological bold relief is both consistent and logical in racist terms, for the so-called Black matriarch is a kind of folk character largely fashioned by whites out of half truths and lies about the involuntary conditions of black women.

The misuse of the term matriarch has led many people to identify any woman present in a household where no male resides a matriarch. Although anthropologists disagree about whether or not matriarchal societies ever really existed, an examination of available information about the supposed social structure of matriarchies proves without any doubt that the social status of the matriarch was in no way similar to that of black women in the United States. Within the matriarchal society woman was almost always economically secure. The economic situation of black women in United States has never been secure. While the average median income of employed black men has in recent years often surpassed the average median income of white females, the wages black women receive on the average remain considerably lower than that of both white females and black males. The matriarch was most often the owner of property. Since black women receive on the average low or middle incomes, only a few individuals are able to secure and hold property. Within the woman-centered society, the matriarch assumes the authoritative role in government and home life. Anthropologist Helen Diner found in her research on matriarchs that the position of the woman was like that of the man in patriarchal society. Commenting on the matriarchal role, Diner states, "If one sees her perform heavy labor while the male lounges or putters about the house, it is because he is not permitted to perform or decide important things."

Although white sociologists would have all Americans believe that the black female is often the "man of the house," this is rarely the case. Even in single-parent homes, black mothers may go so far as to delegate the responsibility of being the "man" to male children. In some single-parent homes where no male is present, it is acceptable for a visiting male friend or lover to assume a decision-making role. Few black women, even in homes where no men are present, see themselves as adopting a "male" role. Concurrently in American political life few black women exercise decision-making power. While it is true that in contemporary times more black women can be seen in the political arena than ever before in history, in proportion to the population of black women this number is relatively small. The Joint Center for Political Studies located in Washington D.C. reported on the extent to which sexism and racism have led to under-representation of black women in government, and their study revealed:

> Black females in America have more than doubled their presence among elected officials in the four years since 1969. Yet, even today, they account for only about 12% of black elected officials and are an "infinitesimally" small percentage of the elected office holders in the nation the survey revealed. The report continues by saying there are about seven million black women of voting age in the country, but they hold only 336 of the more than 520,000 elective offices in the country. Yet the total number of black women office holders today represent about 160% increase over their number four years ago.

Many features that anthropologists claim characterize matriarchal social structure resemble privileges and rights feminists are fighting to obtain. One such feature of matriarchal society was the complete control women had over their bodies. Diner asserts, "Above all the woman possessed free disposition over her body and may interrupt pregnancy whenever she wishes or prevent it all together." The inability of women in modern society to gain control over their bodies in regards to childbirth has been a primary impetus behind the women's liberation movement. Lower class women and consequently many black women have the least control over their bodies. In most states, women with enough money, (particularly upper and middle class white women), have always been able to rid themselves of unwanted pregnancies. It has been poor women, black and white, who have had the fewest opportunities to exercise control over their reproductive activities. Diner cities many other characteristics common to matriarchal societies which in no way parallel patterns of behavior common to black women. Studying the preferred sex of children in the matriarchal culture, Diner found, "Female children are preferred because they continue the family which boys cannot." Black women, like most women in patriarchal societies prefer the birth of sons, as our society esteems the male child and often ignores or berates the female child. In the female-dominated state, domestic work was considered degrading to the woman just as it is considered beneath the male's dignity in a male-dominated society. Black women perform most of the domestic work in their own homes and in the homes of others. Marriage in the matriarchal state offered women the same privileges rewarded to men in the patriarchal state. Diner contends:

> In marriage obedience is demanded of the male as was specified in the marriage contracts of ancient Egypt. He also must remain faithful, while the wife remains unencumbered. She also retains the right of divorce and repudiation.

Black women have been restricted in these areas as have most women in patriarchal societies.

As is obvious, this cursory comparison of the status of matriarchs with that of black women reveals few similarities. Although various people have written essays and articles that discredit the theory that a black matriarchy exists, the term continues to be widely used to describe the status of black women. It is readily evoked by those white people who wish to perpetuate negative images of black womanhood. At the onset of the emergence of the matriarchy myth it was used to discredit black women and men. Black women were told that they had overstepped the bonds of femininity because they worked outside the home to provide economic suppoort for their families and that by so doing they had de-masculinized black men. Black men were told that they were weak, effeminate, and castrated because "their" women were laboring at menial jobs.

White male scholars who examined the black family by attempting to see in what ways it resembled the white family structure were confident that their data was not biased by their own personal prejudices against women assuming an active role in family decision-making. But it must be remembered that these white males were educated in an elite institutional world that excluded both black people and many white women, institutions that were both racist and sexist. Consequently, when they observed black families, they chose to see the independence, will power, and initiative of black women as an attack on the masculinity of black men. Their sexism blinded them to the obvious positive benefits to both black men and women that occurred when black females assumed an active role in parenting. They argued that the black woman's performance of an active role in family life both as mothers and providers had deprived black men of their patriarchal status in the home. And this argument was used to explain the large numbers of female-headed households, the assumption being that black men had vacated their parenting roles because of domineering black women, whose dominance was attributed to their being economic providers while black men were unemployed.

The belief that men naturally want to provide for the economic well-being of their families and therefore feel de-masculinized if unemployment or low wages prevent them from so doing seems an out-of-place and totally false assumption in a society where men are taught to expect rewards for their provision. The structure of marriage in patriarchal society is based on a system of exchange, one in which men are traditionally taught to provide economically for women and children in exchange for sexual, housekeeping, and nurturing services. The argument that black men have been emasculated because they were not always able to assume the patriarchal role of provider is based on the assumption that black men feel that they should provide for their families and therefore feel unmanned or guilty if they cannot do so. Yet such an assumption does not appear to be based on actual fact. In many homes, black men who are employed are not eager to give money to wives and children and are even resentful that they are expected to share hard-earned low wages with others. Concurrently, despite the fact that the American capitalist economic structure forces many black men to be unemployed, there are some black men who would rather not work "shit" jobs with endless hassles and little monetary reward if they can survive without them; these men do not have doubts about their masculinity. To many of them a low paying menial job is more an attack on their masculinity than no job at all. While I do not mean to imply that there have not been large numbers of black men concerned with being providers, it is important that we remember that the desire to provide is not an innate male instinct.

Surveys of groups of women from all races and classes who attempt to get child care payments from ex-husbands would provide ample evidence of the reluctance of men to assume provider roles. It is more likely that lower-middle and middle class black men who have absorbed standard definitions of masculinity would feel that it is important to provide economically for families and consequently feel ashamed, even de-masculinized if unable to assume the provider role. But at the time of the emergence of the matriarchy myth as popular social theory, the great majority of black men were working class. And among working class men, who are by definition the recipients of low wages and who almost always have difficulty providing for families, achievement of manhood or masculine status is not determined solely on the basis of economics.

An ignorant person hearing an analysis of the black matriarchy theory might easily assume that the jobs black women were able to acquire which enabled them to be providers elevated their status above that of black men, but that was never the case. In actuality many of the service jobs black women were employed to perform forced them into daily contact with racist whites who abused and humiliated them. They may have suffered much more intensely a feeling of being de-humanized and degraded than unemployed black men who stood on street corners all day long. Being employed at a low paying job does not necessarily lead to a positive self-concept. It may very well be that unemployed black men were able to maintain a personal dignity that black women employed in service jobs were forced to surrender in their work arena. I can certainly remember lower class black men in our neighborhood commenting on the fact that some jobs were not worth doing because of the loss of one's personal dignity, whereas black women were made to feel that when survival was the crucial issue, personal dignity should be sacrificed. The black female who thought herself "too good" to do domestic work or other service jobs was often ridiculed for being uppity. Yet everyone sympathized when unemployed black men talked about their inability to accept "the man" bossing them. Sexist thinking made it acceptable for black men to refuse menial work even if they were unable to provide for family and children. Many black men who deserted family and children were not regarded contemptuously even though such behavior on the part of black women would have been condemned.

The argument that black women were matriarchs was readily accepted by black people even though it was an image created by white males. Of all the negative stereotypes and myths that have been used to characterize black womanhood, the matriarchy label has had the greatest impact on the consciousness of many black people. The independent role black women were obliged to play both in the labor force and in the family was automatically perceived as unladylike. Negative attitudes toward working women have always existed in American society and black men were not unique in regarding black women workers with disapproval. Robert Smuts, in his general study of female workers (a study that is primarily concerned with white women), *Women and Work in America*, discussed the types of attitudes toward working women that were once the norm in American society:

> In the decades before and after the turn of the century, the employment of women was a major public issue. Like the judges of the Wisconsin Court, many Americans felt that it was akin to treason for a woman to want to work. Most of the arguments advanced to support this position were based on a common conception of the nature and role of women. In physique, temperament and mentality, the argument ran, women are exquisitely specialized for their functions as mothers and guardians of the home. To employ a woman in other ways would endanger not only her essential female qualities but also her sanity, her health, and even her life. This view of woman implied a complementary view of man. As the man was deficient in the feminine ideals of "tenderness, compassion... beauty and the harmonies of grace" essential to the creation of a true home; but abundantly endowed with the masculine qualities of "energy, desire, daring, and forcible possession" necessary in the world of business, government, and war...

While this is a perfect example of racist scholarship, in that the women that Smuts is talking about entering the work force for the first time are white women, it does provide an accurate picture of the negative attitudes toward women in the labor force.

Just as white men perceived the entry of white women into the labor force as a threat to male positions and masculinity, black men were socialized to regard the presence of black women in the labor force with similar suspicions. The matriarchy theory gave the black male a framework on which to base his condemnation of working black women. Many black men who did not feel at all personally de-masculinized absorbed sexist ideology and regarded wage-earning black women with contempt. These men claimed that the female-headed household was a direct result of the matriarchal tendencies of black women and argued that no "real" man could remain in a household where he was not the sole boss. Using this sexist logic, we can safely assume that it was never the black female having so much power in the home that alienated some black men, but that she had any power at all. Those male scholars who label a domestic worker who slaves away forty hours a week and earns enough money for food, rent, and other necessary expenses as financially independent do her a grave disservice. For most men in sexist society, being the boss is synonymous with having absolute power. In patriarchal homes men are likely to feel threatened even if women have a babysitting job that provides them extra grocery money. Black men were able to use the matriarchy myth as a psychological weapon to justify their demands that black women assume a more passive subservient role in the home.

Those men who accepted the myth that black women were matriarchs did regard black females as a threat to their personal power. Such thinking is not at all peculiar to black men. Most men in a patriarchal society fear and resent women who do not assume traditional passive roles. By shifting the responsibility for the unemployment of black men onto black women and away from themselves, white racist oppressors were able to establish a bond of solidarity with black men based on mutual sexism. White men preyed upon sexist feelings impressed upon the black male psyche from birth to socialize black men so that they would regard not all women, but specifically black women as the enemies of their masculinity. I have previously mentioned that historiographers who study black people's history tend to minimize the oppression of black females and concentrate their attention on black men. Despite the fact that black women are victims of sexist and racist oppression, they are usually depicted as having received more advantages than black men in American history, a fact that cannot be substantiated by historical evidence. The matriarchy myth suggested that once again black women had been granted privileges denied black men. Yet even if white people had been eager to hire black men in service jobs to work as maids and washermen, such jobs would have been refused because they would have been regarded as an assault on male dignity. White sociologists presented the matriarchy myth in such a way that it implied black women had "power" in the family and black men had none, and although these conclusions were based solely on data concerned with economic status, they fostered divisiveness between black men and women.

Some black women have been as willing to accept the matriarchy theory as have black men. They were eager to identify themselves as matriarchs because it seemed to them that black women were finally receiving acknowledgement of their contribution to the black family. Young black women interested in African history were attracted to the theory that a matriarchy existed in America because they had learned that woman-ruled societies existed in our mother land, so they claimed matriarchy as an African cultural retention. In general, many black women were proud to be labeled matriarchs because the term had many more positive implications than other labels used to characterize black womanhood. It was certainly more positive than mammy, bitch, or slut. If we were matriarchs, feelings of honor and pride would be in order, but as the social status of black women in the United States is far from being matriarchal, the motivation of white and black people who persistently label black women matriarchs must be questioned. Just as whites used the myth that all black women were sexually loose as a way to devalue black womanhood, they used the matriarchy myth to impress upon the consciousness of all

Americans that black women were masculinized, castrating, ball-busters.

Yet black women embraced the label matriarch because it allowed them to regard themselves as privileged. This merely indicates how effectively colonizers are able to distort the reality of the colonized so that they embrace concepts that actually do them more harm than good. One of the oppressive tactics white slavers used to prevent rebellions and slave uprisings was the brainwashing of slaves to believe that black people were really better taken care of as slaves than they would be as free people. Black slaves who accepted their master's picture of freedom were afraid to break the bonds of slavery. A similar tactic has been used to brainwash black women. White colonizers encourage black women, who are economically oppressed and victimized by sexism and racism, to believe that they are matriarchs, that they exercise some social and political control over their lives.

Once black women are deluded and imagine that we have power we don't really possess, the possibility that we might organize collectively to fight against sexist-racist oppression is reduced. I interviewed a black woman usually employed as a clerk who was living in near poverty, yet she continually emphasized the fact that black woman was matriarchal, powerful, in control of her life; in fact she was nearly having a nervous breakdown trying to make ends meet. Significantly, sociologists who label black women matriarchs never discussed woman's social status within the matriarchal state, for if they had, black folks would have known immediately that it in no way resembled the lot of black women. Without a doubt, the false sense of power black women are encouraged to feel allows us to think that we are not in need of social movements like a women's movement that would liberate us from sexist oppression. The sad irony is of course that black women are often most victimized by the very sexism we refuse to collectively identify as an oppressive force.

The myth of the black matriarchy helped to further perpetuate the image of black women as masculinized, domineering, amazonic creatures. The black female was depicted by whites as an Amazon because they saw her ability to endure hardships no "lady" was supposedly capable of enduring as a sign that she possessed an animalistic sub-human strength. This belief was perfectly compatible with ideas about the nature of black womanhood that emerged during the 19th century. Like the matriarchy myth, the belief that black women were amazonic was largely based on myth and fantasy. Traditional Amazons were a collective group of women who joined together in an effort to promote female self-government. Unlike matriarchs, Amazons were interested in building societies in which the male figure would be present in only small numbers. Diner writes of Amazonic women:

> Amazons deny the man, destroy the male progeny, concede no separate existence to the active principle, reabsorb it, and develop it in themselves in androgynous fashion female on the left, male on the right.... Homer developed the right feeling for the Amazons when he called them anitianeirai, which may be interpreted as "man hating" or as "mannish."

The great majority of women interviewed for this book were eager to acknowledge the feeling that the most important aspect of a woman's life was her relationship with a man. Perusal of *Essence* magazine reveals that there is almost an obsessive concern among black women with male-female relationships.

Most black women have not had the opportunity to indulge in the parasitic dependence upon the male that is expected of females and encouraged in patriarchal society. The institution of slavery forced black women to surrender any prior dependence on the male figure and obliged them to struggle for their individual survival. The social equality that characterized black sex role patterns in the work sphere under slavery did not create a situation that allowed black women to be passive. Despite sexist myths about the inherent weakness of women, black women have had to exert a certain independence of spirit because of their presence in the work force. Few black women have had a choice as to whether or not they will become workers. And participation of black women in the work force has not led to the formation of a feminist consciousness. Though many black women entered the labor force in service areas, in agriculture, in industry, and in clerical work, most of them resented the fact that they were not being supported economically by men. In recent years, attitudes toward women entering the work force have radically changed. Many women either want to work or face the reality that they must be employed to make ends meet. The rise in middle class white women workers who enter the work force in ever increasing numbers indicates a change in attitudes toward working women. Until it was accepted that most women, black or white, would be in the capitalist work force, many black women bitterly resented the circumstances that forced them to work. It is interesting that white women were criticized and persecuted when they first entered the American work force in large numbers, but after the initial attacks ceased there was little protest. And there has been no discussion of them having become masculinized as a result of performing tasks traditionally done by men.

When white women enter the work force today it is seen as a positive step, a move toward gaining independence, while more than ever before in our history black women who enter the work force are encouraged to feel that they are taking jobs from black men or de-masculinizing them. For fear of undermining the self-confidence of black men, many young college-educated black women repress their own career aspirations. While black women are often forced by circumstances to act in assertive ways, most black women I talked with as preparation for this book believed men were superior to women and that a degree of submission to male authority was a necessary part of woman's role. The stereotypical image of the black woman as strong and powerful so dominates the consciousness of most Americans that even if a black woman is clearly conforming to sexist notions of femininity and passivity she may be characterized as tough, domineering, and strong. Much of what has been perceived by whites as an Amazonic trait in black women has been merely stoical acceptance of situations we have been powerless to change.

While the matriarchy myth and the myth of the black amazon have as their core ingredient an image of woman as active, powerful being, the stereotypical image of Aunt Jemima depicted the black woman as passive, longsuffering, and sub-missive. Historian Herbert Gutman argues that there is little evidence to support the notion:

> ...that the typical house servant was an aged mammy who remained in her antebellum place out of loyalty to a white family or because whites had a special concern for such women.

He suggests that the black female nanny in the white household was usually a young black woman with few if any attachments of her own. Gutman does not speculate about the origins of the black mammy figure, but she too was a creature of white imagination. It is not really important that there are black women who resemble the mammy stereotype, it is important that white people created an image of black womanhood which they could tolerate that in no way resembled the great majority of black women. If as Gutman argues the "nanny" in a typical antebellum white household was young and unattached, it is significant that white people have gone to such great lengths to create just the opposite image. It is not too difficult to imagine how whites came to create the black mammy figure. Consi-dering white male lust for the bodies of black females, it is likely that white women were not pleased with young black women working in their homes for fear that liaisons between them and their husbands might be formed, so they conjured up an image of the ideal black nanny. She was first and foremost asexual and consequently she had to be fat (preferably obese); she also had to give the impression of not being clean so she was the wearer of a greasy dirty headrag; her too tight shoes from which emerged her large feet were further confirmation of her bestial cow-like quality. Her greatest virtue was of course her love for white folk whom she willingly and passively served. The mammy image was portrayed with affection by whites because it epitomized the ultimate sexist-racist vision of ideal black womanhood—complete submission to the will of whites. In a sense whites created in the mammy figure a black woman who embodied solely those characteristics they as colonizers wished to exploit. They saw her as the embodiment of woman as passive nurturer, a mother figure who gave all without expectation of return, who not only acknowledged her inferiority to whites but who loved them. The mammy as portrayed by whites poses no threat to the existing white patriarchal social order for she totally submits to the white racist regime. Contemporary television shows continue to present black mammy figures as prototypes of acceptable black womanhood.

The counterpart to the Aunt Jemima images are the Sapphire images. As Sapphires, black women were depicted as evil, treacherous, bitchy, stubborn, and hateful, in short all that the mammy figure was not. The Sapphire image had as its base one of the oldest negative stereotypes of woman—the image of the female as inherently evil. Christian mythology depicted woman as the source of sin and evil; racist-sexist mythology simply designated black women the epitome of female evil and sinfulness. White men could justify their de-humanization and sexual exploitation of black women by arguing that they possessed inherent evil demonic qualities. Black men could claim that they could not get along with black women because they were so evil. And white women could use the image of the evil sinful black woman to emphasize their own innocence and purity. Like the biblical figure Eve, black women became the scapegoats for misogynist men and racist women who needed to see some group of women as the embodiment of female evil. In an essay in *The Black Woman*, Perry and Bond describe Sapphire as she was and is depicted in American culture:

> Movies and radio shows of the 1930's and 1940's invariably pedaled the Sapphire image of the black woman: she is depicted as iron-willed, effectual, treacherous toward and contemptible of black men, the latter being portrayed as simpering, ineffectual whipping boys. Certainly, most of us have encountered domineering Black females (and white ones too). Many of them have been unlucky in life and love and seek a bitter haven from their disappointments in fanatical self-sufficiency.

The Sapphire image was popularized by the radio and television show *Amos 'n' Andy*, in which Sapphire is the nagging, shrewish wife of Kingfish. As the title indicates, the show focused on the black male characters. Sapphire's shrewish personality was used primarily to create sympathy in viewers for the black male lot. The Sapphire identity has been projected onto any black woman who overtly expresses bitterness, anger, and rage about her lot. Consequently, many black women repress these feelings for fear of being regarded as shrewish Sapphires. Or they embrace the Sapphire identity as a reaction to the harsh treatment of black women in society. The "evilness" of a given black woman may merely be the facade she presents to a sexist-racist world that she realizes would only exploit her if she were to appear vulnerable.

All the myths and stereotypes used to characterize black womanhood have their roots in negative anti-woman mythology. Yet they form the basis of most critical inquiry into the nature of black female experience. Many people have difficulty appreciating black women as we are because of eagerness to impose an identity upon us based on any number of negative stereotypes. Widespread efforts to continue devaluation of black womanhood make it extremely difficult and oftentimes impossible for the black female to develop a positive self-concept. For we are daily bombarded by negative images. Indeed, one strong oppressive force has been this negative stereotype and our acceptance of it as a viable role model upon which we can pattern our lives.

3

The Imperialism
of Patriarchy

When the contemporary movement toward feminism began, there was little discussion of the impact of sexism on the social status of black women. The upper and middle class white women who were at the forefront of the movement made no effort to emphasize that patriarchal power, the power men use to dominate women, is not just the privilege of upper and middle class white men, but the privilege of all men in our society regardless of their class or race. White feminists so focused on the disparity between white male/white female economic status as an indication of the negative impact of sexism that they drew no attention to the fact that poor and lower-class men are as able to oppress and brutalize women as any other group of men in American society. The feminist tendency to make synonymous male possession of economic power with being an oppressor caused white men to be labeled "the" enemy. The labeling of the white male patriarch as "chauvinist pig" provided a convenient scapegoat for black male sexists. They could join with white and black women to protest against white male oppression and divert attention away from their sexism, their support of patriarchy, and their sexist exploitation of women. Black leaders, male and female, have been unwilling to acknowledge black male sexist oppression of black women because they do not want to acknowledge that racism is not the only oppressive force in our lives. Nor do they wish to complicate efforts to resist racism by acknowledging that black men can be victimized by racism but at the same time act as sexist oppressors of black women. Consequently there is little acknowledgement of sexist oppression in black male/female relationships as a serious problem. Exaggerated emphasis on the impact of racism on black men has evoked an image of the black male as effete, emasculated, crippled. And so intensely does this image dominate American thinking that people are absolutely unwilling to admit that the damaging effects of racism on black men neither prevents them from being sexist oppressors nor excuses or justifies their sexist oppression of black women.

Black male sexism existed long before American slavery. The sexist politics of white-ruled and colonized America merely reinforced in the minds of enslaved black people existing beliefs that men were the superiors of women. In an earlier discussion of the slave sub-culture I noted that the patriarchal social structure gave the enslaved male higher status than the enslaved female. Historiographers have not been willing to acknowledge either the higher status of the enslaved male in the black sub-culture or the fact that sex-based differentiation of work roles as assigned by white masters reflected a bias towards the male (i.e., black women required to perform "male" tasks but black men not required to perform "female" tasks—women labor in fields but men do no childcare). In modern times, the emphasis on the sexist definition of the male role as that of protector and provider has caused scholars to argue that the most damaging impact of slavery on black people was that it did not allow black men to assume the traditional male role. But the inability of black men to assume the role of protector and provider did not change the reality that men in patriarchal society automatically have higher status than women—they are not obliged to earn that status. Consequently, the enslaved black male, though obviously deprived of the social status that would enable him to protect and provide for himself and others, had a higher status than the black female slave based solely on his being male. This higher status did not always lead to preferential treatment but it was overtly acknowledged by sex-role differentiation.

Sexist discrimination against all women in the labor force and in higher educational spheres throughout 19th century America meant that of those black people who aspired to leadership roles, either during slavery or at manumission, black men were the more likely candidates. As black men dominated leadership roles, they shaped the early black liberation movement so that it reflected a patriarchal bias. Courageous black women leaders like Sojourner Truth and Harriet Tubman did not represent the norm; they were exceptional individuals who dared to challenge the male vanguard to struggle for freedom. At public appearances, rallies, luncheons, and dinners black male leaders spoke in support of patriarchal rule. They did not talk directly about discriminating against women. Their sexism was shrouded in romantic visions of black men lifting black women to pedestals. Outspoken black nationalist leader Martin Delaney in his political treatise, *The Condition, Elevation, Emigration, and Destiny of the Colored People of the United States*, which was first published in 1852, advocated distinct sex role patterns for black women and men:

> Let our young men and women prepare themselves for usefulness and business; that the men may enter into merchandise, trading, and other things of importance; the young women may become teachers of various kinds, and otherwise fill places of usefulness....
>
> Our females must be qualified, because they are to be the mothers of our children. As mothers are the first nurse and instructors of children; from them children consequently, get their first impression, which being always the most lasting, should be the more correct. Raise the mothers above the level of degradation, and the offspring is elevated with them. In a word, instead of our young men, transcribing in their blank books recipes for Cooking, we desire to see them making the transfer of Invoices and Merchandise.

Frederick Douglass saw the entire racial dilemma in America as a struggle between white men and black men. In 1865 he published an essay titled "What the Black Man Wants" which argued in favor of black men gaining the vote while women remained disenfranchised:

> Shall we at this moment justify the deprivation of the Negro of the right to vote, because some one else is deprived of that privilege? I hold that women, as well as men, have the right to vote, and my heart and my voice go with the movement to extend suffrage to women; but the question rests on another basis than that on which our rights rest. We may be asked, I say, why we want it. I will tell you why we want it. We want it because it is our right, first of all. No class of men can, without insulting their own nature, be content with any deprivation of their rights.

It is evident in this statement that to Douglass the "negro" was synonymous with the black male. And though he claims in his essay to support woman suffrage, he clearly believed it was more appropriate and fitting that men be given the right to vote. By emphasizing that the right to vote was more important to men than women, Douglass and other black male activists allied themselves with white male patriarchs on the basis of shared sexism.

In their private lives, black male activists and political leaders demanded that their wives assume subordinate roles. Black woman feminist Mary Church Terrell recorded in her diary that her activist lawyer husband desired her to play no role in political affairs. She complained that he treated her as if she were a fragile glass object in need of constant protection. Terrell's husband used his patriarchal status to sabotage her political work. His fear was that her femininity would be "tarnished" by too many encounters with the world outside the home. The marriage of Booker T. Washington and his third wife, Margaret Murray, was fraught with similar conflict. Margaret wanted to assume a more active role in the black political movement but was encouraged to confine herself to the domestic sphere. While Ida B. Wells' husband supported her political work, she did not abdicate responsibility for child care and on various occasions appeared at speaking engagements with her small children. In 1894 Calvin Chase wrote an editorial in the

Bee entitled "Our Women" in which he urged black men to assume the role of protector of black womanhood. Chase admonished, "Let us do our duty in defending our women; let us set up a system of reformation not only of our women but everything that pertains to the race's advancement." Nineteenth century black male leaders like James Forten, Charles Remond, Martin Delaney, and Frederick Douglass supported the efforts of women to gain political rights but they did not support social equality between the sexes. They were in fact adamant in their support of patriarchal rule. Like white male liberals in the 19th century, black male leaders were not against granting women access to political rights as long as men remained the acknowledged superior authorities. In a discussion of southern etiquette as regards attitudes toward women, one white writer noted, "Southern racists and black activists looked at women in similar terms. Both viewed the female as a second sex with distinctly limited privileges."

Among the 19th century black masses, folks were wholeheartedly committed to establishing and maintaining a patriarchal social order in their segregated culture. Black women wanted to assume the "feminine" role of homemaker supported, protected, and honored by a loving husband. There was one problem—few jobs available to black men. Racist whites refused black men employment, while black women were able to find domestic service jobs. White and black people have interpreted white employment of black women in domestic service jobs while refusing to provide jobs for black men as an indication that they favored black women over black men. Such thinking ignores the obvious fact that domestic service jobs (maids, housekeepers, washerwomen) were not regarded as either "real" work or meaningful labor. White people did not perceive black women engaged in service jobs as performing significant work that deserved adequate economic reward. They saw domestic service jobs performed by black women as being merely an extension of the "natural" female role and considered such jobs valueless. While white men could feel threatened by competition from black males for sound wage-earning jobs and use racism to exclude black men, white women were eager to surrender household chores to black female servants. Since household chores were seen as degrading work, it is unlikely that white people were showing favoritism to black women by allowing them these jobs. It is more likely that they thought black women, whom they believed were without dignity and self-respect, would feel no shame in doing menial labor.

Although many black women worked outside the home, they remained staunch supporters of patriarchy. They regarded the black male who could not free them from the labor force with hostility, anger, and contempt. Even in some homes where black men worked but did not earn enough money to be the sole provider, black wives were bitter about having to enter the work force. Much of the tension in black marriages and other male-female relationships was caused by black females' pressuring men to assume the breadwinner, head-of-the-household role. Often black men were not as upwardly mobile as black women wanted them to be. As women in capitalist America are the major consumers, much of the pressure on all men to earn more money is imposed upon them by women. And black women have been no exception. Unlike many white men who responded to the materialistic demands of wives by becoming devoted disciples of the cult of work, many black men reacted with hostility to such demands. Other black men worked two or three jobs to provide for the materialistic demands of wife and children.

In 1970, L.J. Axelson published an essay, "The Working Wife: Difference in Perception Among Negro and White Males," which introduced data that showed black men were much more supportive and accepting of their wives being in the work force than white men. Often it has been black women who have been the most angered and enraged about black men not assuming the provider role. The 1968 issue of the *Liberator* published an essay by black woman writer Gail Stokes titled "Black Woman to Black Man." In the essay she expressed hostility and contempt for those black men who were reluctant to assume the provider role:

> Of course you will say, "How can I love you and want to be with you when I come home and you're looking like a slob? Why, white women never open the door for their husbands the way you black bitches do."

I should guess not, you ignorant man. Why should they be in such a state when they've got maids like me to do everything for them? There is no screaming at the kids for her, no standing over the hot stove; everything is done for her, and whether her man loves her or not, he provides... provides... do you hear that, nigger? PROVIDES!

The rage of working black women, who have equated manhood with the ability of men to be sole economic providers in the family, and who consequently feel cheated and betrayed by black men who refuse to assume these roles, is but another indication of the extent of their acceptance and support of patriarchy. They saw the black male who did not eagerly assume the breadwinner role as selfish, lazy, and irresponsible, or in white male sociological terms, "emasculated." Their perception of the black male as weak or effeminate is not an indication that they have repudiated male dominance; it is an acknowledgement on their part that they wholeheartedly embrace patriarchy and feel contemptuous toward black men who have no desire to assume the breadwinner role.

The idea that black men felt emasculated because black women worked outside the home is based on the assumption that men find their identity through work and are personally fulfilled by acting as breadwinners. Such an assumption does not reveal any consideration of the fact that the vast majority of jobs men perform are time-consuming, uninteresting, and energy-draining—and are not the least bit personally fulfilling. Myron Brenton, author of *The American Male—A Penetrating Look at the Masculinity Crisis*, argues that men do not feel that work allows them to assert "masculine power." While he admits that most American men are socialized by sexism to regard work as their role, he argues that the men who accept the idea that work is an expression of their masculine power and should be the most important aspect of their life experience are usually disappointed. He comments, "The American male looks to his breadwinner role to confirm his manliness, but work itself is fraught with de-humanizing—i.e., unmanning—influence." Black men in America have rarely romanticized labor, largely because they have for the most part performed less desirable tasks. They knew that performing jobs society deemed menial with bosses and supervisors harassing and persecuting them was not fulfilling. They also knew that the monetary rewards for their labor rarely compensated for the indignities they were forced to endure. Ambitious black men who absorbed the values of middle class white patriarchs have been most eager to accept the emasculation theory, as they are the men who feel most crippled by the racial hierarchy in American society that has traditionally denied black men unlimited access to power. It is common to hear famous black male celebrities or other financially successful black men lament the "powerlessness of the black male" or stress that he is unable to be a "real" man in American society. They choose to ignore the reality that their own successes are an indication that black men are not totally trapped, crippled, or emasculated. In actuality, what they are really saying is that they have embraced patriarchy and with it male competitiveness, and that as long as white men dominate capitalist power structures in American society, black men will feel emasculated.

Many black men who express the greatest hostility toward the white male power structure are often eager to gain access to that power. Their expressions of rage and anger are less a critique of the white male patriarchal social order and more a reaction against the fact that they have not been allowed full participation in the power game. In the past, these black men have been most supportive of male subjugation of women. They hoped to gain public recognition of their "manhood" by demonstrating that they were the dominant figure in the black family.

Just as 19th century black male leaders felt that it was important that all black men show themselves willing to be protectors and providers of their women as a sign to the white race that they would tolerate no more denial of their masculine privilege, 20th century black male leaders used this same tactic. Marcus Garvey, Elijah Muhammed, Malcolm X, Martin Luther King, Stokely Carmichael, Amiri Baraka and other black male leaders have righteously supported patriarchy. They have all argued that it is absolutely necessary for black men to relegate black women to a subordinate position both in the political sphere and in home life. Amiri Baraka published an essay in the July 1970 issue of *Black World* that publicly announced his commitment to establishing a black patriarchy. Yet he did not use terms like patriarchy or male rule; instead he discussed the formation of a black male-dominated household with its inherent anti-woman stance as if it were a positive reaction against white racist values. His romantic rhetoric was typical of the language black male leaders used to mask the negative implication of their sexist message. Addressing himself to all black people, Baraka asserts:

> We talk about the black woman and the black man like we were separate because we have been separated, our hands reach out for each other, for the closeness, the completeness we are for each other, the expansion of consciousness that we provide for each other. We were separated by the deed and process of slavery. We internalized the process, permitting it to create an alien geography in our skulls, a wandering spirit that had us missing each other, and never never understanding just what it was. After we were gone from each other. My hand might rest on yours, and still you would be gone. And I, of course, not there, out wandering, among the rogues and whores of the universe.

> And so this separation is the cause of our need for self consciousness, and eventual healing. But we must erase the separateness by providing ourselves with healthy African identities. By embracing a value system that knows of no separation but only of the divine complement the black woman is for her man. For instance we do not believe in the "equality" of men and women. We cannot understand what the devils and the devilishly influenced mean when they say equality for women. We could never be equals... nature has not provided thus. The brother says, "Let a woman be a wo-man... and let a man be a ma-an..."

Although Baraka presents this "new" black nation he envisions as a world that will have distinctly different values from those of the white world he is rejecting, the social structure he conceived was based on the same patriarchal foundation as that of white American society. His statements about woman's role were not unlike those white men were expressing at this same period in American history. White males interviewed for the book *The American Male* expressed concern that the growing presence of white women in the work force was threatening their masculine status, and expressed sentimental feelings of longing for the old days when sex-role patterns were more sharply delineated. Like Baraka, they comment:

> Those were the days, all right. A man was a man, and a woman was a woman, and each of them knew what that meant. Father was the head of the family in the real sense of the term. Mother respected him for it and received all the gratifications she needed or wanted at home, doing her well-defined jobs.... Man was strong, woman was feminine—and there was little loose talk about phony equality.

It is no mere coincidence that at the same time white men were expressing doubts and anxieties about their masculine role, black men chose to publicly proclaim that they had subjugated black women. Finally, the black man who had seen himself as the loser in the all male competitive struggle with white men for status and power could show a trump card—he was the "real" man because he could control "his" woman. Baraka and other black men could label white men effeminate and non-masculine. In *Home*, Baraka includes an essay called "american sexual reference: black man" which begins with the homophobic statement:

> Most American white men are trained to be fags. For this reason it is no wonder their faces are weak and blank, left without the hurt that really makes—anytime. That red flush, those silk blue faggot eyes.... Can you, for a second, imagine the average middle-class white man able to do somebody harm? Without the technology that at this moment still has him rule the world? Do you understand the softness of the white man, the weakness, and again the estrangement from reality.

Ironically, the "power" of black men that Baraka and others celebrated was the stereotypical, racist image of the black man as primitive, strong, and virile. Although these same images of black men had been evoked by racist whites to support the argument that all black men were rapists, they were now romanticized as positive characteristics. The American public was impressed by Baraka and others like him who heralded the emergence of black manhood. They reacted to groups like the Black Muslims with their emphasis on strong black manhood with fear, but also with awe and respect.

From their writings and speeches, it is clear that most black political activists of the 60s saw the black liberation movement as a move to gain recognition and support for an emerging black patriarchy. When critics of the black power movement argued that a contradiction of values emerged from black men who espoused black power while at the same time choosing white female companions, they were informed that "real" men demonstrated their power by dating whomever they pleased. When Baraka was asked if a militant black man could have a white female companion he responded:

> Jim Brown put it pretty straight and this is really quite true. He says that there are black men and white men, then there are women. So you can indeed be going through a black militant thing and have yourself a woman. The fact that she happens to be black or white is no longer impressive to anybody, but a man who gets himself a woman is what's impressive. The battle is really between white men and black men whether we like to admit it that is the battlefield at this time.

Black men were announcing via the Black Power movement that they were determined to gain access to power even if it entailed breaking from mainstream American society and setting up a new black sub-culture. White male patriarchs were alarmed by the assertions of militant black men whom they knew had every justifiable reason to be angry, hostile, revengeful, and they reacted with violent resistance. Despite the fact that they were able to resist and defeat black militants, white men were impressed by the sight of black men wearing the badge of their newly affirmed manhood. The Black Power movement had a great impact on the psyches of white Americans. Joel Kovel argues in *White Racism: A Psychohistory* that the black power movement completely changed white perceptions of black people. He contends:

> Through open defiance, encouraged by leaders such as Malcolm X and his radical successors, blacks have cleansed the symbol of blackness, stripped it of its accumulated false

humility, and have in effect proceeded toward the regeneration of their own symbolic matrix based upon a positive concept of blackness. That this return to dignity has been possible at all, is a testimonial to the strength of humanity to resist oppression, and a great sign of hope for black and white alike. That it should have to become real through anger and destruction may seem deplorable, but it is unhappily necessary under the crushing terms of the Western symbolic matrix that would not, could not, itself grant humanity to those who had once been property. Here, in this heroic act, is a real break in the endlessly destructive dialectic of our matrix.

Many white men responded favorably to the demands of black power advocates with their emphasis on restoring black men their lost masculinity precisely because their sexism enabled them to identify sympathetically with this cause. The patriarchal privileges black men demanded in the name of black power were precisely the longings sexist patriarchal white men could empathize with. While white men and women could not identify and sympathize with the black race that they had exploited for economic gain demanding reparations, they could easily relate to the desire of black men to assert their "manhood." As Americans, they had not been taught to really believe that social equality was an inherent right all people possess, but they had been socialized to believe that it is the nature of males to desire and have access to power and privilege. In Michele Wallace's controversial book, *Black Macho and the Myth of the Super Woman*, she dismisses the black power movement as ineffectual and suggests that black men were primarily interested in gaining access to the bodies of white women. She fails to understand that the 60s black movement did not merely eradicate many of the barriers that prevented inter-racial dating; it led to numerous social and economic gains for black people. However, the meaningful gains of the black power movement do not either justify or lessen the negative impact of anti-woman attitudes that emerged in much black power rhetoric.

While the 60s black power movement was a reaction against racism, it was also a movement that allowed black men to overtly announce their support of patriarchy. Militant black men were publicly attacking the white male patriarchs for their racism but they were also establishing a bond of solidarity with them based on their shared acceptance of and commitment to patriarchy. The strongest bonding element between militant black men and white men was their shared sexism—they both believed in the inherent inferiority of woman and supported male dominance. Another bonding element was the black male's acknowledgement that he, like the white male, accepted violence as the primary way to assert power. White men reacted to black male violence with the excitement and glee men have traditionally expressed when going to war. Although they attacked black militants, they respected them for their show of force. Since the 60s black power movement, white men have more readily accepted black men on police forces and in more leadership positions in the armed forces. It has been traditionally acceptable for men to put aside their racist feelings in those spheres where men bond on the basis of their sexuality. Despite overt racism in the sports arena, it is there that black men were first able to gain a degree of positive recognition of their masculine prowess. Racism has always been a divisive force separating black men and white men, and sexism has been a force that unites the two groups.

Men of all races in America bond on the basis of their common belief that a patriarchal social order is the only viable foundation for society. Their patriarchal stance is not simply an acceptance of a social etiquette based on discrimination against women; it is a serious political commitment to maintaining political regimes throughout the United States and the world that are male-dominated. John Stoltenberg discusses the political structure of patriarchy in his essay "Toward Gender Justice" published in a book of readings, *For Men Against Sexism.* In his essay he describes characteristic features of patriarchy:

> Under patriarchy, men are the arbiters of identity for both males and females, because the cultural norm of human identity is, by definition, male identity—masculinity. And, under patriarchy, the cultural norm of male identity consists in power, prestige, privilege, and prerogative as over and against the gender class women. That's what masculinity is. It isn't something else.

Attempts have been made to defend this norm of masculinity as having a natural basis in male sexual biology. It has been said for example, that male power in the culture is a natural expression of a biological tendency in human males toward sexual aggression. But I believe that what is true is the reverse. I believe that masculinist genital functioning is an expression of male power in the culture. I believe that male sexual aggression is entirely learned behavior, taught by a culture which men entirely control. I believe, as I will explain, that there is a social process by which patriarchy confers power, prestige, privilege, and prerogative on people who are born with cocks, and that there is a sexual program promoted by the patriarchy (not Mother Nature) for how those cocks are supposed to function.

Stoltenberg also emphasizes that patriarchy is maintained by male bonding on the basis of shared sexism:

The social process whereby people born with cocks attain and maintain masculinity takes place in male bonding. Male bonding is institutionalized learned behavior whereby men recognize and reinforce one another's bona fide membership in the male gender class and whereby men remind one another that they were not born women. Male bonding is political and pervasive. It occurs whenever two males meet. It is not restricted to all-male-groupings. It is the form and content of each and every encounter between two males. Boys learn very early that they had better be able to bond. What they learn in order to bond is an elaborate behavioral code of gestures, speech, habits and attitudes, which effectively exclude women from the society of men. Male bonding is how men learn from each other that they are entitled under patriarchy to power in the culture. Male bonding is how men get that power, and male bonding is how it is kept. Therefore, men enforce a taboo against unbonding—a taboo which is fundamental to patriarchal society.

Racism has not allowed total bonding between white and black men on the basis of shared sexism, but such bonding does occur.

The black male quest for recognition of his "manhood" in American society is rooted in his internalization of the myth that simply by having been born male, he has an inherent right to power and privilege. When racism prevented black people from attaining social equality with whites, black men responded as if they were the sole representatives of the black race and therefore the sole victims of racist oppression. They saw themselves as the people who were being denied their freedom, and not black women. In all his protest fiction, black novelist Richard Wright emphasized the de-humanizing effects of racism on black men as if black women were in no way affected. In his short story "Long Black Song" the hero Silas who has just killed a white man cries out in his rage:

> The white folks ain never gimme a chance! They ain never give no black man a chance! There ain nothing in yo whole life yuh kin keep from em! They take yo lan! They take yo freedom! They take yo women! N then they take yo life!

Wright relegates women to the position of property—they become for him merely an extension of the male ego. His attitude is typical of patriarchal male thinking about women.

Black men are able to dismiss the sufferings of black women as unimportant because sexist socialization teaches them to see women as objects with no human value or worth. This anti-woman attitude is endemic to patriarchy. In Leonard Schein's essay "All Men Are Misogynists," he argues that patriarchy encourages men to hate women:

> Patriarchy's foundation is the oppression of women. The cement of this foundation is the socialization of men to hate women.
>
> Looking at our development as males, it is easy to see how misogyny originates. As young children, our first attraction is to our mother, a woman. As we grow older, we learn to transfer our love for our mother to an identification with our father.
>
> The patriarchal nuclear family makes all its members dependent upon the male (father-husband). It is in this oppressive atmosphere that we grow up, and are extremely sensitive to this hierarchy of power even as children. We realize, more than adults know, that our father (and society in his image, from policeman to doctor to president) is powerful, and that our mother is powerless. She has to scheme and manipulate through sympathy to get what she wants.

Racism does not prevent black men from absorbing the same

sexist socialization white men are inundated with. At very young ages, black male children learn that they have a privileged status in the world based on their having been born male; they learn that this status is superior to that of women. As a consequence of their early sexist socialization, they mature accepting the same sexist sentiments their white counterparts accept. When women do not affirm their masculine status by assuming a subordinate role, they express the contempt and hostility they have been taught to feel toward non-submissive women.

Black men have been sexist throughout their history in America, but in contemporary times that sexism has taken the form of outright misogyny—undisguised woman-hating. Cultural changes in attitudes toward female sexuality have affected male attitudes toward women. As long as women were divided into two groups, virgin women who were the "good" girls and sexually permissive women who were the "bad" girls, men were able to maintain some semblance of caring for women. Now that the pill and other contraceptive devices give men unlimited access to the bodies of women, they have ceased to feel that it is at all necessary to show women any consideration or respect. They can now see all women as "bad," as "whores," and openly reveal their contempt and hatred. As a group, white men expose their hatred by increased exploitation of women as sex objects to sell products and by their wholehearted support of pornography and rape. Black men expose their hatred by increased domestic brutality (white men also) and their vehement verbal denouncement of black women as matriarchs, castraters, bitches, etc. That black men should begin to see the black woman as their enemy was perfectly logical given the structure of patriarchy. Schien writes of male hatred of women:

> ... Psychologically, we objectify the people we hate and consider them our inferiors...

> A second situation which feeds on, deepens, and solidifies our hatred of women develops a little later in time. We begin to realize our privileged position in society as males. The Orthodox Jew prays to God every morning thanking

"Him" that he was not born a woman. Subconsciously we intuit that our privilege can only be maintained if women are kept "in their place." So we live in constant fear, as the threat to our power is everywhere (even, and especially, in our bedroom). This fear of the challenge to our power explains our paranoid hatred toward the "Uppity Woman."

Black women have always been regarded as "too uppity." White men decided this during slavery. When Moynihan first published his report on the black family in 1965 perpetuating the emasculation theory, black men responded initially by exposing the weaknesses and flaws in his argument. They first argued that his assertion that they were emasculated was ridiculous and untrue but it was not long before they began to make the same complaint. Their endorsement of the idea that black women were castraters of men allowed them to bring out of the closet misogynist attitudes. While they embraced on one hand the matriarchy myth and used it to urge black women to be more submissive, on the other hand they communicated the message that their manhood was not threatened by black women because they could always use brute force and physical prowess to subjugate them.

It has always been acknowledged in lower class black communities that the ability to act as breadwinners was not the standard black men used to measure their masculine status. As one black man stated:

> In white society, respect is to a large degree institutionalized. You must respect a man because he is a judge or a professor or a corporate executive. In the ghetto without the institutionalization of respect, a man must earn respect by his own personal qualities, including the ability to defend himself physically.

It is true that white men have institutionalized respect, but their success as men in power is measured by their ability to use technological force to do violence to others, or their ability to exploit others for capitalist ends. So in that sense, their way of acquiring respect for their masculine status is not that different from that of black men. While white men demonstrate their "masculine power" by organizing and implementing the slaughter of Japanese people or Vietnamese people, black men kill one another, or black women. One of the leading causes of death among young black men is black-on-black homicide. Black psychiatrist Alvin Pouissant argues that these black men are "victims of their own self-hatred." While insecure feelings about their selfhood may motivate black men to commit violent acts, in a culture that condones violence in men as a positive expression of masculinity, the ability to use force against another person—i.e., oppress them—may be less an expression of self-hatred than a rewarding, fulfilling act.

In many black communities, young men coming of age feel that they must show their male peers that they are fearless— that they are not afraid of violent acts. Carrying a gun and being prepared to use it are the ways they publicly assert their "masculine" strength. In an imperialist racist patriarchal society that supports and condones oppression, it is not surprising that men and women judge their worth, their personal power, by their ability to oppress others. Recently, a white male journalist for a leading California newspaper reported with shock and outrage that black youths in Cleveland cheered when the slain body of an FBI agent who was murdered by a young black male was brought from a tenement building. Yet in a culture where the cult of violence dominates media (television, films, comic books), it is perfectly understandable that young men and women glorify violence. And in the case of young black males who learn from this same media that they are the automatic targets for white male aggression, it is not surprising that they should feel satisfaction when they see a symbol of white law enforcement murdered by a peer. After all, sexist socialization has been encouraging them all their lives to feel they are "unmanned" if they cannot commit violent acts.

It is often forgotten that the very same Moynihan report that promoted the idea that black men had been "unmanned" by black women urged black men to enter military service. Moynihan called war an "utterly masculine world," and it was in this world of killing that he imagined black men would develop personal confidence and pride. Like other white male patriarchs he endorsed violence as a positive expression of male strength. He argued:

> Given the strains of the disorganized and matrifocal family life in which so many Negro youths come of age, the armed forces are a dramatic and desperately needed change: a world away from woman, a world run by strong men of unquestioned authority.

Sexism fosters, condones, and supports male violence against women, as well as encouraging violence between males. In patriarchal society, men are encouraged to channel frustrated aggression in the direction of those without power—women and children. And white men and black men alike abuse women. While the interests of this book motivate me to be more concerned with black male misogyny, I do not intend to imply that black males epitomize sexist oppression in our society. There has always been greater emphasis on the violent acts of black men in American society, as it diverts attention away from white male violence. Male violence against women has increased in America in the last twenty years. Anti-feminists argue that changing sex role patterns have threatened males so that they are demonstrating their anger by domestic brutality. As supporters of male dominance they assert that violent acts against women will continue until society returns to the good old-fashioned days of sharply delineated sex roles.

While feminist supporters like to think that feminism has been the motivating force behind changes in woman's role, in actuality changes in the American capitalist economy have had the greatest impact on the status of women. More women than ever before are in America's work force not because of feminism but because families can no longer rely on the income of the father. Feminism has been used as a psychological tool to make women think that work they might otherwise see as boring, tedious, and time consuming is liberating. For whether feminism exists or not, women must work. Overt misogynist attacks on women occured long before the feminist movement, and most women who bear the brunt of male aggression and brutality today are not feminists. Much of the violence against women in this culture is promoted by the capitalist patriarchy that encourages men to see themselves as privileged while daily stripping them of their humanity in de-humanizing work, and as a consequence men use violence against women to restore their lost sense of power and masculinity. Media brainwashing encourages men to use violence as a way to subjugate women. In effect, modern patriarchy restructured to meet the needs of advanced capitalism eradicated earlier romanticized versions of the male hero role as a strong knight, protecting and providing for the damsel in distress, and replaced it by worship of the rapist, the macho man, the brute who uses force to get his demands met.

In the 60s, black men disassociated themselves from chivalrous codes of manhood that at one time taught males to deplore the use of violence against women, and idolized those men who exploited and brutalized women. Amiri Baraka dramatized his acceptance of violence as a way to subjugate women in his play *Madheart*. In a scene where a black woman is urging the black man to leave white women alone and come to her, the black male "hero" of the play demonstrates his power to use force to subdue her:

BLACK MAN: I'll get you back. If I need to.

WOMAN (laughs): You need to, baby... just look around you. You better get me back, if you know what's good for you... you better.

BLACK MAN (looking around at her squarely, he advances): I better?... (a soft laugh) Yes. Now is where we always are... that now... (he wheels and suddenly slaps her crosswise, back and forth across the face.)

WOMAN: Wha??? What... oh love... please... don't hit me. (he hits her, slaps her again.)

BLACK MAN: I want you woman, as a woman. Go down. (He slaps her again) Go down, submit, submit... to love... and to man, now forever.

WOMAN (weeping, turning her head from side to side): Please don't hit me... please... (She bends.) The years are so long, without you, man, I've waited... waited for you...

BLACK MAN: And I've waited.

WOMAN: I've seen you humbled, black man, seen you crawl for dogs and devils.

BLACK MAN: And I've seen you raped by savages and beasts, and bear bleach-shit children of apes.

WOMAN: You permitted it... you could... do nothing.

BLACK MAN: But now I can (he slaps her... drags her to him, kissing her deeply on the lips.) That shit is ended, woman, you with me, and the world is mine.

Baraka did not celebrate this male violence against women in isolation. His plays were performed before audiences of women and men who were not shocked, disgusted, and outraged by what they saw. While Baraka in the 60s used drama to act out scenes of male oppression of women, in the 70s a black woman was actually murdered on stage by a black male playwright. Black woman poet Audre Lorde refers to this murder in a short essay, "The Great American Disease" in which she comments on black male woman-hating. She recalls the case of Pat Cowan:

> She was a young black actress in Detroit, 22 years old and a mother. She answered an ad last spring for a black actress to audition in a play called "Hammer." As she acted out an argument scene, watched by the playwright's brother and her son, the black male playwright picked up a sledgehammer and bludgeoned her to death from behind.

Most men in patriarchal society, though fanatically committed to male dominance, like to think that they will not use brutality to oppress women. Yet at very young ages male children are socialized to regard females as their enemy and as a threat to their masculine status and power—a threat, however, they can conquer through violence. As they grow older they learn that aggression toward women lessens their anxiety and fear that their masculine power will be usurped. In his essay on misogyny, Schien concludes:

> We must understand that our anger (and hatred) is something that comes from within us. It is not woman's fault. It is the attitude that patriarchal society has encouraged us to feel toward all women. When finally confronted with the reality of feminism, which threatens our power and privileges, our defenses cannot hide our true anger and we turn to incredible violence.

> We have to accept that this anger belongs to us and stems from our hatred of women. I know men say that they really do not hate women, they have just treated them unfairly because of socialization ("Those other men are rapists, not me."). This can be a cop-out and untruth. All men do hate women, and until we take responsibility for our personal hatred, we will not be able to seriously explore our emotionality nor treat women as equal human beings.

Black women are one of the most devalued female groups in American society, and thus they have been the recipients of a male abuse and cruelty that has known no bounds or limits. Since the black woman has been stereotyped by both white and black men as the "bad" woman, she has not been able to ally herself with men from either group to get protection from the other. Neither group feels that she deserves protection. A sociological study of low income black male-female relationships showed that most young black men see their female companions solely as objects to be exploited. Most boys in the study referred to black women as "that bitch" or "that whore." Their perception of the black female as a degraded sexual object is similar to white male perceptions of the black female. Often in black communities the male who overtly reveals his hatred and contempt of women is admired. The contemporary glorification of male violence against women has caused the pimp, once a despised figure in communities, to be elevated to the status of hero. The pimp's misogynist treatment of women was romanticized in movies like *Sweet Sweetback* or *Cool World*, and in books like *Iceberg Slim* that glorified his exploits. Much of Malcolm X's very fine autobiography is devoted to a retelling of his days as a pimp. He tells readers that he felt comfortable in the role of pimp because he saw women as the enemies of masculinity who must be triumphed over through exploitation. While he repudiated the role of pimp after he became a Muslim, it is presented simply as a distorted expression of his quest for "manhood."

In 1972 Christina and Richard Milner published a book entitled *Black Players* in which they romanticize and glorify the lives of pimps. One section of the book is called "Male Dominance—Men Have to Control" which emphasizes to the reader that the pimp impresses others by his subjugation of the female. The Milners contend:

> First and foremost, the pimp must be in complete control of his women; this control is made conspicuous to others by a series of little rituals which express symbolically his woman's attitude. When in the company of others she must take special pains to treat him with absolute deference and respect. She must light his cigarettes, respond to

his every whim immediately and never, never, contradict him. In fact, a ho's strictly not supposed to speak in the company of pimps unless spoken to.

The role pimps expected women to play is merely an imitation of the role patriarchs expect their wives and daughters to play. The passive subordinate demeanor expected of the prostitute is not unlike that demanded of all women in patriarchal society.

Black men who joined the Black Muslim groups in the sixties and seventies were committed to sexist role patterns. In his first-hand report of the Black Muslim movement *Black Nationalism*, published in 1962, E.U. Essien-Udom noted that the black men who joined the Muslims were those who accepted the "feminine ideal" as woman's natural role. Essien-Udom observed:

> Muslim women appear to accept their men as 'first among equals,' and in theory, at least, regard the man as the breadwinner and the head of the family. The Muslim women address the men as 'sir.' Wives address husbands similarly.

It was understood in the Muslim love relationship that the woman would defer to the man on all occasions. Many black women were eager to join the Muslims because they wanted black men to act in a dominant role. Like other black liberation groups, the Black Muslims glorified manhood and at the same time relegated women to the status of a subordinate.

Malcolm X was the Black Muslim leader that many people saw as an exemplary figure of black manhood, but it is impossible to read his autobiography without becoming aware of the hatred and contempt he felt toward women for much of his life. Toward the middle of the book Malcolm writes of the black woman he has married:

> I guess by now I will say I love Betty. She's the only woman I ever even thought about loving. And she's one of the very few—four women—whom I have ever trusted. The thing is, Betty's a good Muslim woman and wife...
>
> Betty... understands me. I would even say I don't imagine many other women might put up with the way I am. Awakening this brainwashed black man and telling this

arrogant, devilish white man the truth about himself, Betty understands, is a full-time job. If I have work to do when I am home, the little time I am at home, she lets me have the quiet I need to work in. I'm rarely at home more than half of any week; I have been away as much as five months. I never get much chance to take her anywhere and I know she likes being with her husband. She is used to my calling her from airports anywhere from Boston to San Francisco, or Miami to Seattle, or, here lately, cabling her from Cairo, Accra, or the Holy City of Mecca.

While Malcolm extolled the virtues of his wife, his general attitude toward women was extremely negative.

An important aspect of the Black Muslim movement for many of its members was its puritanical emphasis on purifying and cleansing black people, in particular black women, of their unclean sexuality. In American patriarchy, all women are believed to embody sexual evil. Sexual racism has caused black women to bear the brunt of society's need to degrade and devalue women. While white women have been placed on a symbolic pedestal, black women are seen as fallen women. In the black community the fair-skinned black woman who most nearly resembled white women was seen as the "lady" and placed on a pedestal while darker-skinned black women were seen as bitches and whores. Black men have shown the same obsessive lust and contempt for female sexuality that is encouraged throughout our society. Because they, like white men, see black women as inherently more sexual and morally depraved than other groups of women, they have felt the greatest contempt toward her. Within the Muslim movement, the black man who had once looked upon black women as devalued property could suddenly see her as elevated to the status of respected wife and mother, that is, after she wrapped her head in cloth and covered her body in long skirts and dresses.

Essein-Udom reported that most black women were motivated to join the Muslim movement by the promise that they would be respected by black men. He calls this section "The Negro Women: Journey from Shame" and comments:

> One of the principal motives which lead Negro women to join the Nation is their desire to escape from their position

as women in Negro subculture... Womanly virtues are respected in the Nation. The Muslim male's attitude toward, and treatment of, Negro women contrasts sharply with the disrespect and indifference with which lower-class Negroes treat them. Muhammad's semireligious demand that his followers must respect the black woman has an appeal for black women seeking to escape from their lowly and humiliating position in Negro society and from the predatory sex ethos of the lower-class. A refuge from these abuses is found in the Nation of Islam, and freedom from sex exploitation. It is a journey from shame to dignity.

Black women entering the Nation of Islam were treated with greater respect than they were accustomed to prior to their conversion, but this better treatment did not happen because Muslim black men had changed their basic negative attitudes toward women. It happened because their male leader Elijah Muhammad decided that it would be in the movement's interest to develop a strong patriarchal base in which women were given protection and consideration in exchange for submission. In many cases, Black Muslim men, who treated black women within the movement with respect, continued to abuse and exploit non-Muslim women. Like white men, their labeling of one group of women as "good" necessitated the labeling of another group as "bad." The black male's move to idealize black womanhood was not unlike white male idealization of white women during the 19th century. Whereas white men elevated white female status by labeling black women sluts and whores, 20th century black Muslim men elevated black females by labeling white women she-devils and whores. In both cases neither group of men could surrender their belief that women are inherently evil. They maintained their contemptuous attitudes toward women but simply channeled them in a specific direction.

A number of non-Muslim black men who regarded black women as devalued property sought white female companions. Black men's idealization of white womanhood is as rooted in sexist woman-hating as is their devaluation of black womanhood. In both cases, women are still being reduced to the level of objects. The idealized woman becomes property, symbol, and ornament; she is stripped of her essential human qualities. The devalued woman becomes a different kind of object; she is the spittoon in which men release their negative anti-woman feelings. Those black men who believe deeply in the American dream, which is in essence a masculine dream of dominance and success at the expense of others, are most likely to express negative feelings about black women and positive feelings about white women. It is not surprising that the black male who finds self-affirmation on the terms set forth by white men would desire a white woman. Because he is living every moment of his life in competition with white men, he must also compete for the woman the white male has decided best represents "Miss America."

The popular notion that black men desire white women because they are so much more "feminine" than black women has been used to place responsibility for black male desire for white female companions onto black women. In sexist terms, if black men are rejecting black women and seeking other companions, then surely black women must be doing something wrong since men are always right. The truth is—in sexist America, where women are objectified extensions of male ego, black women have been labeled hamburger and white women prime rib. And it is white men who have created this race-sex hierarchy, not black men. Black men merely accept and support it. In fact, if white men decided at any given moment that owning a purple female was the symbol of masculine status and success, black men in competition with white men would have to try and possess a purple female. While I believe it is perfectly normal for people of different races to be sexually attracted to one another, I do not think that black men who confess to loving white women and hating black women or vice versa are simply expressing personal preferences free of culturally socialized biases.

Black men have been eager to present their desire to "possess" white women as an attempt to overcome racial dehumanization. In *Sex and Racism in America*, Calvin Hernton contends:

> In America, however, where the Negro is the underdog and the white woman is the great symbol of sexual purity and

pride, the black man is often driven to pursue her in lieu of aggrandizing his lack of self-esteem. Having the white woman, who is the prize of our culture, is a way of triumphing over a society that denies the Negro his basic humanity.

Note that Hernton continually uses the word "Negro" when he is in fact referring solely to black men. All too often black men have tried to argue (and in many cases have successfully convinced their audience) that their objectification of white females has some direct correlation to the degree to which they are oppressed in American society. This logic enables them to mask the basic anti-woman feeling that stimulates their lust to possess white women. Many black men who date and marry white women have positive self-concepts and have achieved a certain measure of capitalist status and success. Their desire for white companions is less an indication of how brutalized they are by white racism and more an expression of the fact that their successes mean little if they cannot also possess that human object white patriarchal culture offers to men as the supreme reward for masculine achievement.

Few black men who discuss black male/white female relationships question why it is black men do not seek to challenge the values of that white patriarchy that encourages them to objectify and if possible exploit white women. Instead they present the black male as a "victim," one who is unable to resist the societal seduction that teaches him to de-humanize black women through devaluation and de-humanize white women through idealization. In actuality, black men do not resist the efforts of white male advertisers and public relations people who encourage them to objectify all women, and in particular white women, because to do so would be to challenge patriarchy and its oppression of women. The black male's assertion that "possessing" a white woman is a triumph over racism is a false truth that masks the reality that his acceptance of her as "the" symbol of status and success is primarily an indication of the extent to which he supports and accepts patriarchy. In their eagerness to gain access to the bodies of white women, many black men have shown that they were far more concerned with exerting masculine privilege than challenging racism. Their behavior is not unlike that of white male patriarchs who, on one hand, claimed to be white supremacists, but who could not forego sexual contact with the women of the very race they claimed to hate. What this indicates is that as men, they place the exertion of masculine privilege above all else in life. And if it is necessary for them to abuse and exploit women in order to maintain that privilege, they will do so without hesitation.

Often in feminist writing, women express bitterness, rage, and anger about male oppressors because it is one step that helps them to cease believing in romanticized versions of sex-role patterns that deny woman's humanity. Unfortunately, our over-emphasis on the male as oppressor often obscures the fact that men too are victimized. To be an oppressor is de-humanizing and anti-human in nature, as it is to be a victim. Patriarchy forces fathers to act as monsters, encourages husbands and lovers to be rapists in disguise; it teaches our blood brothers to feel ashamed that they care for us, and denies all men the emotional life that would act as a humanizing, self-affirming force in their lives. The old notion of the patri-arch who is worthy of respect and honor has long had no place in an advanced capitalist world. Since patriarchy has become merely a sub-heading under the dominant system of imperialist capitalism, as patriarchs men do not serve their families and communities but serve the interests of the State. Consequently they are not affirmed in their domestic lives. As one psycho-therapist emphasizes in *The American Male*:

> He may have been a big hero in high school—president of the student body or a star athlete, that sort of thing. But then he gets out into the world, and he becomes a cog in the organization, and he comes home feeling defeated.

Men are encouraged to phobically focus on women as their ENEMY so that they will blindly allow other forces—the truly powerful de-humanizing elements in American life—to strip them daily of their humanity. The select group of patriarchal women (who support and uphold patriarchal ideology) and patriarchal men who shape American capitalism have in fact made sexism into a commodity that they can sell while at the same time brainwashing men to feel that personal identity, worth and value, can be obtained through the oppression of women, and that is the ultimate weapon by which patriarchs keep men in states of submission.

Commenting on black female/male relationships, one writer asserts:

> Self-hatred and violence seethe in black sexual relationships. Because of this, black men and women rarely experience natural love in their relating—they get sex and no love or they get love and no sex. The love quality, plus the quality of respect for females is impoverished by the pimp/whore syndrome imposed for so long upon black people by American racism and oppression. Violence masquerades as affection. The deeper, more binding emotions of male and female are mutilated via mutual exploitation, distrust, disrespect and strivings for selfish aggrandizement. In fact, there are thousands and thousands of young and old blacks who know of no other mode, who have no other conception of what a man/woman relationship is except that of sex, money, automobiles, and male/female politics ("war of the sexes") vehicled by violence, physical or verbal, or both.

This writer sees the negative tensions that exist between black women and men as being solely motivated by "American racism and oppression." This over-emphasis on racism as the explanation for black female/male problems in relationships blinds us to the reality that sexism has as grave an impact on our modes of relating. The unwillingness of many black people to acknowledge that sexism fosters and perpetuates violence and hatred between men and women is due to their unwillingness to challenge patriarchal social order. Black men and women who support patriarchy and consequently support sexist oppression of women have a tremendous investment in presenting the social situation of black people in such a way that it seems we are only oppressed and victimized by racism.

But let's face it—despite the reality of racist oppression there are other ways that we as black people are victimized in American society. And it is just as important that we be aware of other oppressive forces like sexism, capitalism, narcissism, etc., that threaten our human liberation. It in no way diminishes our concern about racist oppression for us to acknowledge that our human experience is so complex that we cannot understand it if we only understand racism. Fighting against sexist oppression is important for black liberation, for as long as sexism divides black women and men we cannot concentrate our energies on resisting racism. Many of the tensions and problems in black male/female relationships are caused by sexism and sexist oppression. And the black writer who commented on these relationships would have been closer to the mark if he had stated:

> Self-hatred and violence seethe in sexual relationships. Because of this, men and women rarely experience natural love in their relating—they get sex and no love or they get love and no sex. The love quality, plus the quality of respect for females is impoverished by the pimp/whore syndrome imposed for so long upon people by American *patriarchy and sexist oppression.* Violence masquerades as affection. The deeper, more binding emotions of male and female are mutilated via mutual exploitation, distrust, disrespect and strivings for selfish aggrandizement. In fact, there are thousands and thousands of young and old people who know of no other mode, who have no other conception of what a man/woman relationship is except that of sex, money, automobiles, and male/female politics ("war of the sexes") vehicled by violence, physical, or verbal, or both.

Those women and men who feel concerned about the mounting hatred and violence in black female/male relationships come no closer to understanding the actual dynamics of that aggression when they refuse to acknowledge sexism as an oppressive force. Black nationalism, with its emphasis on separatism and forming new cultures, has allowed many black people to think that we have somehow lived in American society for hundreds of years and yet have remained untouched, uninfluenced by the world around us. It is this romanticized notion of our blackness (the myth of the noble savage) that allows many people to refuse to see that the social orders black nationalists have proposed with their foundation of patriarchy would not have changed in any way negative feelings between black women and men. In the name of liberating black folks from white oppressors, black men could present oppression of black women as a strength—a sign of newfound glory. Consequently, black liberation movements have had many positive implications as regards eliminating racist oppression but in no way present programs that are aimed at eliminating sexist oppression. Black female/male relationships (like all male/female relationships in American society) are tyrannized by the imperialism of patriarchy which makes oppression of women a cultural necessity.

As people of color, our struggle against racial imperialism should have taught us that wherever there exists a master/slave relationship, an oppressed/oppressor relationship, violence, mutiny, and hatred will permeate all elements of life. There can be no freedom for black men as long as they advocate subjugation of black women. There can be no freedom for patriarchal men of all races as long as they advocate subjugation of women. Absolute power for patriarchs is not freeing. The nature of fascism is such that it controls, limits, and restricts leaders as well as the people fascists oppress. Freedom (and by that term I do not mean to evoke some wishy-washy hang-loose do-as-you-like world) as positive social equality that grants all humans the opportunity to shape their destinies in the most healthy and communally productive way can only be a complete reality when our world is no longer racist or sexist.

4

Racism and Feminism: The Issue of Accountability

American women of all races are socialized to think of racism solely in the context of race hatred. Specifically in the case of black and white people, the term racism is usually seen as synonymous with discrimination or prejudice against black people by white people. For most women, the first knowledge of racism as institutionalized oppression is engendered either by direct personal experience or through information gleaned from conversations, books, television, or movies. Consequently, the American woman's understanding of racism as a political tool of colonialism and imperialism is severely limited. To experience the pain of race hatred or to witness that pain is not to understand its origin, evolution, or impact on world history. The inability of American women to understand racism in the context of American politics is not due to any inherent deficiency in woman's psyche. It merely reflects the extent of our victimization.

No history books used in public schools informed us about racial imperialism. Instead we were given romantic notions of the "new world," the "American dream," America as the great melting pot where all races come together as one. We were taught that Columbus *discovered* America; that "Indians" were scalphunters, killers of innocent women and children; that black people were enslaved because of the biblical curse of Ham, that God "himself" had decreed they would be hewers of wood, tillers of the field, and bringers of water. No one talked of Africa as the cradle of civilization, of the African and Asian people who came to America before Columbus. No one mentioned mass murders of Native Americans as genocide, or the rape of Native American and African women as terrorism. No one discussed slavery as a foundation for the growth of capitalism. No one described the forced breeding of white wives to increase the white population as sexist oppression.

I am a black woman. I attended all-black public schools. I grew up in the south where all around me was the fact of racial discrimination, hatred, and forced segregation. Yet my education as to the politics of race in American society was not that different from that of white female students I met in integrated high schools, in college, or in various women's groups. The majority of us understood racism as a social evil perpetuated by prejudiced white people that could be overcome through bonding between blacks and liberal whites, through militant protest, changing of laws or racial integration. Higher educational institutions did nothing to increase our limited understanding of racism as a political ideology. Instead professors systematically denied us truth, teaching us to accept racial polarity in the form of white supremacy and sexual polarity in the form of male dominance.

American women have been socialized, even brainwashed, to accept a version of American history that was created to uphold and maintain racial imperialism in the form of white supremacy and sexual imperialism in the form of patriarchy. One measure of the success of such indoctrination is that we perpetuate both consciously and unconsciously the very evils that oppress us. I am certain that the black female sixth grade teacher who taught us history, who taught us to identify with the American government, who loved those students who could best recite the pledge of allegiance to the American flag was not aware of the contradiction; that we should love this government that segregated us, that failed to send schools with all black students supplies that went to schools with only white pupils. Unknowingly she implanted in our psyches a seed of the racial imperialism that would keep us forever in bondage. For how does one overthrow, change, or even challenge a system that you have been taught to admire, to love, to believe in? Her innocence does not change the reality that she was teaching black children to embrace the very system that oppressed us, that she encouraged us to support it, to stand in awe of it, to die for it.

That American women, irrespective of their education, economic status, or racial identification, have undergone years of sexist and racist socialization that has taught us to blindly trust our knowledge of history and its effect on present reality, even though that knowledge has been formed and shaped by an oppressive system, is nowhere more evident than in the recent feminist movement. The group of college-educated white middle and upper class women who came together to organize a women's movement brought a new energy to the concept of women's rights in America. They were not merely advocating social equality with men. They demanded a transformation of society, a revolution, a change in the American social structure. Yet as they attempted to take feminism beyond the realm of radical rhetoric and into the realm of American life, they revealed that they had not changed, had not undone the sexist and racist brainwashing that had taught them to regard women unlike themselves as Others. Consequently, the Sisterhood they talked about has not become a reality, and the women's movement they envisioned would have a transformative effect on American culture has not emerged. Instead, the hierarchical pattern of race and sex relationships already established in American society merely took a different form under "feminism": the form of women being classed as an oppressed group under affirmative action programs further perpetuating the myth that the social status of all women in America is the same; the form of women's studies programs being established with all-white faculty teaching literature almost exclusively by white women about white women and frequently from racist perspectives; the form of white women writing books that purport to be about the experience of American women when in fact they concentrate solely on the experience of white women; and finally the form of endless argument and debate as to whether or not racism was a feminist issue.

If the white women who organized the contemporary movement toward feminism were at all remotely aware of racial politics in American history, they would have known that overcoming barriers that separate women from one another would entail confronting the reality of racism, and not just racism as a general evil in society but the race hatred they might harbor in their own psyches. Despite the predominance of patriarchal rule in American society, America was colonized on a racially imperialistic base and not on a sexually imperialistic base. No degree of patriarchal bonding between white male colonizers and Native American men overshadowed white racial imperialism. Racism took precedence over sexual alliances in both the white world's interaction with Native Americans and African Americans, just as racism overshadowed any bonding between black women and white women on the basis of sex. Tunisian writer Albert Memmi emphasizes in *The Colonizer and the Colonized* the impact of racism as a tool of imperialism:

> Racism appears... not as an incidental detail, but as a consubstantial part of colonialism. It is the highest expression of the colonial system and one of the most significant features of the colonialist. Not only does it establish a fundamental discrimination between colonizer and colonized, a sine qua non of colonial life, but it also lays the foundation for the immutability of this life.

While those feminists who argue that sexual imperialism is more endemic to all societies than racial imperialism are probably correct, American society is one in which racial imperialism supersedes sexual imperialism.

In America, the social status of black and white women has never been the same. In 19th and early 20th century America, few if any similarities could be found between the life experiences of the two female groups. Although they were both subject to sexist victimization, as victims of racism black women were subjected to oppressions no white woman was forced to endure. In fact, white racial imperialism granted all white women, however victimized by sexist oppression they might be, the right to assume the role of oppressor in relationship to black women and black men. From the onset of the contemporary move toward feminist revolution, white female organizers attempted to minimize their position in the racial caste hierarchy of American society. In their efforts to disassociate themselves from white men (to deny connections based on shared racial caste), white women involved in the move toward feminism have charged that racism is endemic to white male patriarchy and have argued that they cannot be held responsible for racist oppression. Commenting on the issue of white female accountability in her essay " 'Disloyal to Civilization': Feminism, Racism, and Gynephobia," radical feminist Adrienne Rich contends:

> If Black and White feminists are going to speak of female accountability, I believe the word racism must be seized, grasped in our bare hands, ripped out of the sterile or defensive consciousness in which it so often grows, and transplanted so that it can yield new insights for our lives and our movement. An analysis that places the guilt for active domination, physical and institutional violence, and the justifications embedded in myth and language, on white women not only compounds false consciousness; it allows us all to deny or neglect the charged connection among black and white women from the historical conditions of slavery on, and it impedes any real discussion of women's instrumentality in a system which oppresses all women and in which hatred of women is also embedded in myth, folklore, and language.

No reader of Rich's essay could doubt that she is concerned that women who are committed to feminism work to overcome barriers that separate black and white women. However, she fails to understand that from a black female perspective, if white women are denying the existence of black women, writing "feminist" scholarship as if black women are not a part of the collective group American women, or discriminating against black women, then it matters less that North America was colonized by white patriarchal *men* who institutionalized a racially imperialistic social order than that white women who purport to be feminists support and actively perpetuate anti-black racism.

To black women the issue is not whether white women are more or less racist than white men, but that they are racist. If women committed to feminist revolution, be they black or white, are to achieve any understanding of the "charged connections" between white women and black women, we must first be willing to examine woman's relationship to society, to race, and to American culture as it is and not as we would ideally have it be. That means confronting the reality of white female racism. Sexist discrimination has prevented white women from assuming the dominant role in the perpetuation of white racial imperialism, but it has not prevented white women from absorbing, supporting, and advocating racist ideology or acting individually as racist oppressors in various spheres of American life.

Every women's movement in America from its earliest origin to the present day has been built on a racist foundation—a fact which in no way invalidates feminism as a political ideology. The racial apartheid social structure that characterized 19th and early 20th century American life was mirrored in the women's rights movement. The first white women's rights advocates were never seeking social equality for all women; they were seeking social equality for white women. Because many 19th century white women's rights advocates were also active in the abolitionist movement, it is often assumed they were anti-racist. Historiographers and especially recent feminist writing have created a version of American history in which white women's rights advocates are presented as champions of oppressed black people. This fierce romanticism has informed most studies of the abolitionist movement. In contemporary times there is a general tendency to equate abolitionism with a repudiation of racism. In actuality, most white abolitionists, male and female, though vehement in their anti-slavery protest, were totally opposed to granting social equality to black people. Joel Kovel, in his study *White Racism: A Psychohistory*, emphasizes that the "actual aim of the reform movement, so nobly and bravely begun, was not the liberation of the black, but the fortification of the white, conscience and all."

It is a commonly accepted belief that white female reformist empathy with the oppressed black slave, coupled with her recognition that she was powerless to end slavery, led to the development of a feminist consciousness and feminist revolt. Contemporary historiographers and in particular white female scholars accept the theory that the white women's rights advocates' feelings of solidarity with black slaves were an indication that they were anti-racist and were supportive of social equality of blacks. It is this glorification of the role white women played that leads Adrienne Rich to assert:

> ... It is important for white feminists to remember that—despite lack of constitutional citizenship, educational deprivation, economic bondage to men, laws and customs forbidding women to speak in public or to disobey fathers, husbands, and brothers—our white foresisters have, in Lillian Smith's words, repeatedly been "disloyal to civilization" and have "smelled death in the word 'segregation'," often defying patriarchy for the first time, not on their own behalf but for the sake of black men, women, and children. We have a strong anti-racist female tradition despite all efforts by the white patriarchy to polarize its creature-objects, creating dichotomies of privilege and caste, skin color, and age and condition of servitude.

There is little historical evidence to document Rich's assertion that white women as a collective group or white women's rights advocates are part of an anti-racist tradition. When white women reformers in the 1830s chose to work to free the slave, they were motivated by religious sentiment. They attacked slavery, not racism. The basis of their attack was moral reform. That they were not demanding social equality for black people is an indication that they remained committed to white racist supremacy despite their anti-slavery work. While they strongly advocated an end to slavery, they never advocated a change in the racial hierarchy that allowed their caste status to be higher than that of black women or men. In fact, they wanted that hierarchy to be maintained. Consequently, the white women's rights movement which had a lukewarm beginning in earlier reform activities emerged in full force in the wake of efforts to gain rights for black people precisely because white women wanted to see no change in the social status of blacks until they were assured that their demands for more rights were met.

White women's rights advocate and abolitionist Abby Kelly's comment, "We have good cause to be grateful to the slave for the benefit we have received to ourselves, in working for him. In striving to strike his irons off, we found most surely, that we were manacled ourselves," is often quoted by scholars as evidence that white women became conscious of their own limited rights as they worked to end slavery. Despite popular 19th century rhetoric, the notion that white women had to learn from their efforts to free the slave of their own limited rights is simply erroneous. No 19th century white woman could grow to maturity without an awareness of institutionalized sexism. White women did learn via their efforts to free the slave that white men were willing to advocate rights for blacks while denouncing rights for women. As a result of negative reaction to their reform activity and public effort to curtail and prevent their anti-slavery work, they were forced to acknowledge that without outspoken demands for equal rights with white men they might ultimately be lumped in the same social category with blacks—or even worse, black men might gain a higher social status than theirs.

It did not enhance the cause of oppressed black slaves for white women to make synonymous their plight and the plight of the slave. Despite Abby Kelly's dramatic statement, there was very little if any similarity between the day-to-day life experiences of white women and the day-to-day experiences of the black slave. Theoretically, the white woman's legal status under patriarchy may have been that of "property," but she was in no way subjected to the de-humanization and brutal oppression that was the lot of the slave. When white reformers made synonymous the impact of sexism on their lives, they were not revealing an awareness of or sensitivity to the slave's lot; they were simply appropriating the horror of the slave experience to enhance their own cause.

The fact that the majority of white women reformers did not feel political solidarity with black people was made evident in the conflict over the vote. When it appeared that white men might grant black men the right to vote while leaving white women disenfranchised, white suffragists did not respond as a group by demanding that all women and men deserved the right to vote. They simply expressed anger and outrage that white men were more committed to maintaining sexual hierarchies than racial hierarchies in the political arena. Ardent white women's rights advocates like Elizabeth Cady Stanton who had never before argued for women's rights on a racially imperialistic platform expressed outrage that inferior "niggers" should be granted the vote while "superior" white women remained disenfranchised. Stanton argued:

> If Saxon men have legislated thus for their own mothers, wives and daughters, what can we hope for at the hands of Chinese, Indians, and Africans?... I protest against the enfranchisement of another man of any race or clime until the daughters of Jefferson, Hancock, and Adams are crowned with their rights.

White suffragists felt that white men were insulting white womanhood by refusing to grant them privileges that were to be granted black men. They admonished white men not for their sexism but for their willingness to allow sexism to overshadow racial alliances. Stanton, along with other white women's rights supporters, did not want to see blacks enslaved, but neither did she wish to see the status of black people improved while the status of white women remained the same.

At the beginning of the 20th century, white women suffragists were eager to advance their own cause at the expense of black people. In 1903 at the National American Woman's Suffrage Convention held in New Orleans, a southern suffragist urged the enfranchisement of white women on the grounds that it "would insure immediate and durable white supremacy." Historian Rosalyn Terborg-Penn discusses white female support of white supremacy in her essay "Discrimination Against Afro-American Women in the Woman's Movement 1830-1920":

As early as the 1890's, Susan B. Anthony realized the potential to the woman suffrage cause in wooing southern white women. She chose expedience over loyalty and justice when she asked veteran feminist supporter Frederick Douglass not to attend the National American Woman Suffrage Association convention scheduled in Atlanta....

During the National American Woman Suffrage Association meeting of 1903 in New Orleans, the *Times Democrat* assailed the association because of its negative attitude on the question of black women and the suffrage for them. In a prepared statement signed by Susan B. Anthony, Carrie C. Catt, Anna Howard Shaw, Kate N. Gordon, Alice Stone Blackwell, Harriet Taylor Upton, Laura Clay, and Mary Coggeshall, the board of officers of the NAWSA endorsed the organization's states' rights position, which was tantamount to an endorsement of white supremacy in most states, particularly in the south.

Racism within the women's rights movement did not emerge simply as a response to the issue of suffrage; it was a dominant force in all reform groups with white female members. Terborg-Penn contends:

> Discrimination against Afro-American women reformers was the rule rather than the exception within the woman's rights movement from the 1830's to 1920. Although white feminists Susan B. Anthony, Lucy Stone, and some others encouraged black women to join the struggle against sexism during the nineteenth century, antebellum reformers who were involved with women's abolitionist groups as well as women's rights organizations actively discriminated against black women.

In their efforts to prove that solidarity existed between 19th century black and white female reformers, contemporary women activists often cite the presence of Sojourner Truth at Women's Rights conventions to support their argument that white female suffragists were anti-racist. But on every occassion Sojourner Truth spoke, groups of white women protested. In *The Betrayal of the Negro*, Rayford Logan writes:

> When the General Federation of Women's Clubs was faced with the question of the color line at the turn of the century, Southern clubs threatened to secede. One of the first

expressions of the adamant opposition to the admission of colored clubs was disclosed by the Chicago *Tribune* and the *Examiner* during the great festival of fraternization at the Atlanta Exposition, the Encampment of the GAR in Louisville, and the dedication of the Chickamauga battlefield.... The Georgia Women's Press Club felt so strongly on the subject that members were in favor of withdrawing from the Federation if colored women were admitted there. Miss Corinne Stocker, a member of the Managing Board of the Georgia Women's Press Club and one of the editors of the *Atlanta Journal*, stated on September 19: "In this matter the Southern women are not narrow-minded or bigoted, but they simply cannot recognize the colored women socially.... At the same time we feel that the South is the colored woman's best friend."

Southern white women's club members were most vehement in their opposition to black women joining their ranks, but northern white women also supported racial segregation. The issue of whether black women would be able to participate in the women's club movement on an equal footing with white women came to a head in Milwaukee at the General Federation of Women's Clubs conference when the question was raised as to whether black feminist Mary Church Terrell, then president of the National Association of Colored Women, would be allowed to offer greetings, and whether Josephine Ruffin, who represented the black organization the New Era Club, would be recognized. In both cases white women's racism carried the day. In an interview in the Chicago *Tribune*, the president of the federation, Mrs. Lowe, was asked to comment on the refusal to acknowledge black female participants like Josephine Ruffin, and she responded: "Mrs. Ruffin belongs among her own people. Among them she would be a leader and could do much good, but among us she can create nothing but trouble." Rayford Logan comments on the fact that white women like Mrs. Lowe had no objection to black women trying to improve their lot; they simply felt that racial apartheid should be maintained. Writing of Mrs. Lowe's attitude toward black women, Logan comments:

Mrs. Lowe had assisted in establishing kindergartens for colored children in the South, and the colored women in charge of them were all her good friends. She associated with them in a business way, but, of course they would not think of sitting beside her at a convention. Negroes were "a race by themselves, and among themselves they can accomplish much, assisted by us and by the federation, which is ever ready to do all in its power to help them." If Mrs. Ruffin were the "cultured lady every one says she is, she should put her education and her talents to good uses as a colored woman among colored women."

Anti-black feelings among white female club members were much stronger than anti-black sentiment among white male club members. One white male wrote a letter to the Chicago *Tribune* in which he stated:

Here we have the spectacle of educated, refined, and Christian women who have been protesting and laboring for years against the unjust discrimination practiced against them by men, now getting together and the first shot out of their reticules is fired at one of their own because she is black, no other reason or pretence of reason.

Prejudices white women activists felt toward black women were far more intense than their prejudices toward black men. As Rosalyn Penn states in her essay, black men were more accepted in white reform circles than black women. Negative attitudes toward black women were the result of prevailing racist-sexist stereotypes that portrayed black women as morally impure. Many white women felt that their status as ladies would be undermined were they to associate with black women. No such moral stigma was attached to black men. Black male leaders like Frederick Douglass, James Forten, Henry Garnett and others were occasionally welcome in white social circles. White women activists who would not have considered dining in the company of black women welcomed individual black men to their family tables.

Given white fear of amalgamation between the races and the history of white male sexual lust for black females, we cannot rule out the possibility that white women were reluctant to acknowledge black women socially for fear of sexual competition. In general, white women did not wish to associate with black women because they did not want to be contaminated by morally impure creatures. White women saw black women as a direct threat to their social standing—for how could they be idealized as virtuous, goddess-like creatures if they associated with black women who were seen by the white public as licentious and immoral? In her speech to the 1895 delegates from black women's clubs, Josephine Ruffin told her audience that the reason white women club members did not want to join with black women was because of the supposed "black female immorality," and she urged them to protest the perpetuation of negative stereotypes about black womanhood:

> All over America there is to be found a large and growing class of earnest, intelligent, progressive colored women who, if not leading full, useful lives, are only waiting for the opportunity to do so, many of them still warped and cramped for lack of opportunity, not only to do more but to be more; and yet, if an estimate of the colored women of America is called for, the inevitable reply, glibly given, is: "For the most part, ignorant and immoral, some exceptions of course, but these don't count."
> ... Too long have we been silent under unjust and unholy charges.... Year after year southern women have protested against the admission of colored women into any national organization on the ground of the immorality of these women, and because all refutation has only been tried by individual work, the charge had never been crushed, as it could and should have been at first.... It is to break this silence, not by noisy protestation of what we are not, but by a dignified showing of what we are and hope to become, that we are impelled to take this step, to make of this gathering an object lesson to the world.

The racism white females felt toward black women was as apparent in the work arena as it was in the women's rights movement and in the women's club movement. During the years between 1880 and World War I, white women's rights activists focused their attention on obtaining for women the right to work in various occupations. They saw work for pay as the way for women like themselves to escape economic dependence on white men. Robert Smut, author of *Women and Work in America* (a work that would be more accurtely titled *White Women and Work in America*), writes:

If a woman could support herself in honor, she could refuse to marry or stay married, except on her own terms. Thus, work was seen by many feminists as an actual or potential alternative to marriage, and consequently, as an instrument for reforming the marriage relationship.

The efforts of white women activists to expand employment opportunities for women were focused exclusively on improving the lot of white women workers, who did not identify with black women workers. In fact, the black woman worker was seen as a threat to white female security; she represented more competition. Relationships between white and black women workers were characterized by conflict. That conflict became more intense when black women tried to enter the industrial labor force and were forced to confront racism. In 1919, a study of black women in industry in New York City was published called *A New Day for the Colored Woman Worker.* The study began by stating:

> For generations Colored women have been working in the fields of the south. They have been the domestic servants of both the south and the north, accepting the position of personal service open to them. Hard work and unpleasant work has been their lot, but they have been almost entirely excluded from our shops and factories. Tradition and race prejudice have played the largest part in their exclusion. The tardy development of the south, and the failure of the Colored women to demand industrial opportunities have added further barriers.... For these reasons, the Colored women have not entered the ranks of the industrial army in the past.
>
> That they are doing so today cannot be disputed. War expediency, for a time at least, partially opened the door of industry to them. Factories which had lost men to the war and White women to the war industries, took on Colored women in their places. The demand for more skilled, semi-skilled and unskilled labor had to be met. The existing immigrant labor supply had already been tapped and the flow of immigration stopped, and semi-skilled White workers were being forced up into the really skilled positions by the labor shortage. Cheap labor had to be recruited from somewhere. For the first time employment bureaus and advertisements inserted the word "Colored" before the word "wanted." Colored women, untried as yet,

were available in large numbers.

Black female workers who entered the industrial labor force worked in commercial laundries, food industries, and the less skilled branches of the needle trades, like the lamp shade industry which depended heavily on the labor of black women. Hostility between black and white female workers was the norm. White women did not want to compete with black women for jobs nor did they want to work alongside black women. To prevent white employers from hiring black females, white female workers threatened to cease work. Often white women workers would use complaints about black women workers as a way of discouraging an employer from hiring them.

White women employed by the federal government insisted that they be segregated from black women. In many work situations separate work rooms, washrooms, and showers were installed so that white women would not have to work or wash alongside black women. The same argument white women club members used to explain their exclusion of black women was presented by white women workers, who claimed black women were immoral, licentious, and insolent. They further argued that they needed the protection of segregation so that they would not catch "Negro" diseases. Some white women claimed to have seen black women with vaginal diseases. In one instance a white woman working in the office of the Recorder of Deeds, Maud B. Woodward, swore out an affidavit asserting:

> That the same toilet is used by whites and blacks, and some of said blacks have been diseased evidence thereof being very apparent; that one negro woman Alexander has been for years afflicted with a private disease, and for dread of using the toilet after her some of the white girls are compelled to suffer mentally and physically.

Competition between black and white women workers for jobs was usually decided in favor of white women. Often black women were forced to accept jobs that were considered too arduous or taxing for white women. In candy factories black women not only wrapped and packed candy, they worked as bakers and in this capacity were constantly lifting heavy trays from table to machine and from machine to table. They were doing "loosening" in tobacco factories, a process formerly done solely by men. Investigators for the New York City Study reported:

> Colored women were found on processes that White women refuse to perform. They were replacing boys at cleaning window shades, work which necessitates constant standing and reaching. They were taking men's places in the dyeing of furs, highly objectionable and injurious work involving standing, reaching, the use of a weighted brush, and ill smelling dye. In a mattress factory they were found replacing men at "baling," working in pairs, wrapping five mattresses together and sewing them up ready for shipment. These women had to bend constantly and lift clumsy 160 pound bales.

In racially segregated work situations black women workers were usually paid a lower wage then white women workers. As there was little if any association between the two groups, black women did not always know of the disparity between their salaries and those of white women. Workers for the New York City study found that most employers refused to pay black women workers as much as white women for doing the same job.

> Throughout the trades, differences in the wages of the Colored and White were unmistakable. While every other Colored woman was receiving less than $10.00 a week, of the White workers only one out of every six was so poorly paid.... A great many employers justified the payment of better wages to White women on the grounds of their greater speed. Foremen in the millinery factories, however, admitted that they paid the Colored workers less, even though they were more satisfactory than the White....
> This wage discrimination seems to have taken three forms. Employers have sometimes segregated the Colored workers, keeping the wage scale of the Colored departments lower than that of similar departments made up of White workers.... A second method has been to deny the Colored the opportunity of competing in piece work, as in the case of the Colored pressers in the needle trades who were paid $10.00 a week on a time rate basis, while the

White pressers averaged $12.00 a week at piece work. The third form of discrimination has been the frank refusal of employers to pay a Colored woman as much as a White woman for a week's work.

As a group, white women workers wanted to maintain the racial hierarchy that granted them higher status in the labor force than black women. Those white women who supported employment of black women in unskilled trades felt they should be denied access to skilled process. Their active support of institutionalized racism caused constant hostility between them and black women workers. To avoid uprisings, many plants chose to hire either one race or the other. In plants where both groups were present, the conditions under which black women worked were much worse than those of white female workers. The refusal of white women to share dressing rooms, bathrooms, or lounge areas with black women often meant that black women were denied access to these comforts. In general black women workers were continually abused because of the racist attitudes of white women workers, and of the white working public as a whole. Researchers for the New York City study summed up their findings by making a plea that more consideration be given the black woman worker in industry:

> It has been apparent throughout this discussion that the coming of the Colored woman into our industries is not without its problems. She is doing work which the White woman is refusing to do, and at a wage which the White woman is refusing the accept. She replaced White women and men and Colored men at a lower wage and is performing tasks which may easily prove to be detrimental to her health. She is making no more mistakes than are common to a new and inexperienced industrial worker, yet she has the greatest of all handicaps to overcome.
> What is the status of the Colored woman in industry with the coming of peace? At the time of greatest need for production and the greatest labor shortage in the history of this country Colored women were the last to be employed: they were not called into industry until there was no other available labor supply. They did the most uninteresting work, the most menial work and by far the most underpaid work....

>   The American people will have to go very far in its
> treatment of the Colored industrial woman to square itself
> with that democratic ideal of which it made so much during
> the war.

Relationships between white and black women were
charged by tensions and conflicts in the early part of the 20th
century. The women's rights movement had not drawn black
and white women close together. Instead, it exposed the fact
that white women were not willing to relinquish their support
of white supremacy to support the interests of all women.
Racism in the women's rights movement and in the work arena
was a constant reminder to black women of the distances that
separated the two experiences, distances that white women did
not want bridged. When the contemporary movement toward
feminism began, white women organizers did not address the
issue of conflict between black and white women. Their
rhetoric of sisterhood and solidarity suggested that women in
America were able to bond across both class and race boundaries—but no such coming together had actually occurred. The
structure of the contemporary women's movement was no
different from that of the earlier women's rights movement.
Like their predecessors, the white women who initiated the
women's movement launched their efforts in the wake of the
60s black liberation movement. As if history were repeating
itself, they also began to make synonymous their social status
and the social status of black people. And it was in the context
of endless comparisons of the plight of "women" and "blacks"
that they revealed their racism. In most cases, this racism was
an unconscious, unacknowledged aspect of their thought, suppressed by their narcissism—a narcissism which so blinded
them that they would not admit two obvious facts: one, that in a
capitalist, racist, imperialist state there is no one social status
women share as a collective group; and second, that the social
status of white women in America has never been like that of
black women or men.

When the women's movement began in the late 60s, it was
evident that the white women who dominated the movement
felt it was "their" movement, that is the medium through

which a white woman would voice her grievances to society. Not only did white women act as if feminist ideology existed solely to serve their own interests because they were able to draw public attention to feminist concerns. They were unwilling to acknowledge that non-white women were part of the collective group women in American society. They urged black women to join "their" movement or in some cases the women's movement, but in dialogues and writings, their attitudes toward black women were both racist and sexist. Their racism did not assume the form of overt expressions of hatred; it was far more subtle. It took the form of simply ignoring the existence of black women or writing about them using common sexist and racist stereotypes. From Betty Friedan's *The Feminine Mystique* to Barbara Berg's *The Remembered Gate* and on to more recent publications like *Capitalist Patriarchy and the Case for Socialist Feminism*, edited by Zillah Eisenstein, most white female writers who considered themselves feminist revealed in their writing that they had been socialized to accept and perpetuate racist ideology.

In most of their writing, the white American woman's experience is made synonymous with *the* American woman's experience. While it is in no way racist for any author to write a book exclusively about white women, it is fundamentally racist for books to be published that focus solely on the American white woman's experience in which that experience is assumed to be *the* American woman's experience. For example, in the course of research for this book, I sought to find information about the life of free and slave black women in colonial America. I saw listed in a bibliography Julia Cherry Spruill's work *Women's Life and Work in the Southern Colonies*, which was first published in 1938 and then again in 1972. At the Sisterhood bookstore in Los Angeles I found the book and read a blurb on the back which had been written especially for the new edition:

> One of the classic works in American social history, *Women's Life and Work in the Southern Colonies* is the first comprehensive study of the daily life and status of women in southern colonial America. Julia Cherry Spruill researched colonial newspapers, court records, and manu-

script material of every kind, drawing on archives and libraries from Boston to Savannah. The resulting book was, in the words of Arthur Schlesinger, Sr., "a model of research and exposition, an important contribution to American social history to which students will constantly turn."

The topics include women's function in the settlement of the colonies; their homes, domestic occupation, and social life; the aims and methods of their education; their role in government and business affairs outside the home; and the manner in which they were regarded by the law and by society in general. Out of a wealth of documentation, and often from the words of colonial people themselves, a vivid and surprising picture—one that had never been seen before—emerges of the many different aspects of these women's lives.

I expected to find in Spruill's work information about various groups of women in American society. I found instead that it was another work solely about white women and that both the title and blurb were misleading. A more accurate title would have been *White Women's Life and Work in the Southern Colonies*. Certainly, if I or any author sent a manuscript to an American publisher that focused exclusively on the life and work of black women in the south, also called *Women's Life and Work in the Southern Colonies*, the title would be automatically deemed misleading and unacceptable. The force that allows white feminist authors to make no reference to racial identity in their books about "women" that are in actuality about white women is the same one that would compel any author writing exclusively on black women to refer explicitly to their racial identity. That force is racism. In a racially imperialist nation such as ours, it is the dominant race that reserves for itself the luxury of dismissing racial identity while the oppressed race is made daily aware of their racial identity. It is the dominant race that can make it seem that their experience is representative.

In America, white racist ideology has always allowed white women to assume that the word woman is synonymous with white woman, for women of other races are always perceived as Others, as de-humanized beings who do not fall under the heading woman. White feminists who claimed to be politically astute showed themselves to be unconscious of the way their use of language suggested they did not recognize the existence of black women. They impressed upon the American public their sense that the word "woman" meant white woman by drawing endless analogies between "women" and "blacks." Examples of such analogies abound in almost every feminist work. In a collection of essays published in 1975 titled *Women: A Feminist Perspective*, an essay by Helen Hacker is included called "Women as a Minority Group" which is a good example of the way white women have used comparisons between "women" and "blacks" to exclude black women and to deflect attention away from their own racial caste status. Hacker writes:

> The relation between women and Negroes is historical, as well as analogical. In the seventeenth century the legal status of Negro servants was borrowed from that of women and children, who were under the patria potestas, and until the Civil War there was considerable cooperation between the Abolitionists and woman suffrage movement.

Clearly Hacker is referring solely to white women. An even more glaring example of the white feminist comparison between "blacks" and "women" occurs in Catherine Stimpson's essay " 'Thy Neighbor's Wife, Thy Neighbor's Servants': Women's Liberation and Black Civil Rights." She writes:

> The development of an industrial economy, as Myrdal points out, has not brought about the integration of women and blacks into the adult male culture. Women have not found a satisfactory way to bear children and to work. Blacks have not destroyed the hard doctrine of their unassimilability. What the economy gives both women and blacks are menial labor, low pay, and few promotions. White male workers hate both groups, for their competition threatens wages and their possible job equality, let alone superiority, threatens nothing less than the very nature of things. The tasks of women and blacks are usually grueling, repetitive, slogging, and dirty....

Throughout Stimpson's essay she makes woman synonymous with white women and black synonymous with black men.

Historically, white patriarchs rarely referred to the racial identity of white women because they believed that the subject of race was political and therefore would contaminate the sanctified domain of "white" woman's reality. By verbally denying white women racial identity, that is by simply referring to them as women when what they really meant was white women, their status was further reduced to that of non-person. In much of the literature written by white women on the "woman question" from the 19th century to the present day, authors will refer to "white men" but use the word "woman" when they really mean "white woman." Concurrently, the term "blacks" is often made synonymous with black men. In Hacker's article she draws a chart comparing the "castelike status of Women and Negroes." Under the heading "Rationalization of Status" she writes for blacks "Thought all right in his place." (?) Hacker's and Stimpson's assumption that they can use the word "woman" to refer to white women and "black" to refer to black men is not unique; most white people and even some black people make the same assumption. Racist and sexist patterns in the language Americans use to describe reality support the exclusion of black women. During the recent political uprisings in Iran, newspapers throughout the U.S. carried headlines that read "Khomeini Frees Women and Blacks." In fact, the American hostages freed from the Iranian Embassy were white women and black men.

White feminists did not challenge the racist-sexist tendency to use the word "woman" to refer solely to white women; they supported it. For them it served two purposes. First, it allowed them to proclaim white men world oppressors while making it appear linguistically that no alliance existed between white women and white men based on shared racial imperialism. Second, it made it possible for white women to act as if alliances did exist between themselves and non-white women in our society, and by so doing they could deflect attention away from their classism and racism. Had feminists chosen to make explicit comparisons between the status of white women and that of black people, or more specifically the status of black women and white women, it would have been more than obvious that the two groups do not share an identical oppression. It would have been obvious that similarities between the status of women under patriarchy and that of any slave or colonized person do not necessarily exist in a society that is both racially and sexually imperialistic. In such a society, the woman who is seen as inferior because of her sex can also be seen as superior because of her race, even in relationship to men of another race. Because feminists tended to evoke an image of women as a collective group, their comparisons between "women" and "blacks" were accepted without question. This constant comparison of the plight of "women" and "blacks" deflected attention away from the fact that black women were extremely victimized by both racism and sexism —a fact which, had it been emphasized, might have diverted public attention away from the complaints of middle and upper class white feminists.

Just as 19th century white woman's rights advocates attempted to make synonymous their lot with that of the black slave was aimed at drawing attention away from the slave toward themselves, contemporary white feminists have used the same metaphor to attract attention to their concerns. Given that America is a hierarchical society in which white men are at the top and white women are second, it was to be expected that should white women complain about not having rights in the wake of a movement by black people to gain rights, their interests would overshadow those of groups lower on the hierarchy, in this case the interests of black people. No other group in America has used black people as metaphors as extensively as white women involved in the women's movement. Speaking about the purpose of a metaphor, Ortega Y Gasset comments:

> A strange thing, indeed, the existence in many of this mental activity which substitutes one thing for another— from an urge not so much to get at the first as to get rid of the second. The metaphor disposes of an object by having it masquerade as something else. Such a procedure would make no sense if we did not discern beneath it an instinctive avoidance of certain realities.

When white women talked about "Women as Niggers," "The

Third World of Women," "Woman as Slave," they evoked the sufferings and oppressions of non-white people to say "look at how bad our lot as white women is, why we are like niggers, like the Third World." Of course, if the situation of upper and middle class white women were in any way like that of the oppressed people in the world, such metaphors would not have been necessary. And if they had been poor and oppressed, or women concerned about the lot of oppressed women, they would not have been compelled to appropriate the black experience. It would have been sufficient to describe the oppression of woman's experience. A white woman who has suffered physical abuse and assault from a husband or lover, who also suffers poverty, need not compare her lot to that of a suffering black person to emphasize that she is in pain.

If white women in the women's movement needed to make use of a black experience to emphasize woman's oppression, it would seem only logical that they focus on the black female experience—but they did not. They chose to deny the existence of black women and to exclude them from the women's movement. When I use the word "exclude" I do not mean that they overtly discriminated against black women on the basis of race. There are other ways to exclude and alienate people. Many black women felt excluded from the movement whenever they heard white women draw analogies between "women" and "blacks." For by making such analogies white women were in effect saying to black women: "We don't acknowledge your presence as women in American society." Had white women desired to bond with black women on the basis of common oppression they could have done so by demonstrating any awareness or knowledge of the impact of sexism on the status of black women. Unfortunately, despite all the rhetoric about sisterhood and bonding, white women were not sincerely committed to bonding with black women and other groups of women to fight sexism. They were primarily interested in drawing attention to their lot as white upper and middle class women.

It was not in the opportunistic interests of white middle and upper class participants in the women's movement to draw attention to the plight of poor women, or the specific plight of black women. A white woman professor who wants the public to see her as victimized and oppressed because she is denied tenure is not about to evoke images of poor women working as domestics receiving less than the minimum wage struggling to raise a family single-handed. Instead it is far more likely she will receive attention and sympathy if she says, "I'm a nigger in the eyes of my white male colleagues." She evokes the image of innocent, virtuous white womanhood being placed on the same level as blacks and most importantly on the same level as black men. It is not simply a coincidental detail that white women in the women's movement chose to make their race-sex analogies by comparing their lot as white women to that of black men. In Catherine Stimpson's essay on women's liberation and black civil rights, in which she argues that "black liberation and women's liberation must go their separate ways," black civil rights is associated with black men and women's liberation with white women. When she writes of the 19th century women's rights movement, she quotes from the work of black male leaders even though black women were far more active in that movement than any black male leader.

Given the psychohistory of American racism, for white women to demand more rights from white men and stress that without such rights they would be placed in a social position like that of black men, not like that of black people, was to evoke in the minds of racist white men an image of white womanhood being degraded. It was a subtle appeal to white men to protect the white female's position on the race/sex hierarchy. Stimpson writes:

> White men, convinced of the holy primacy of sperm, yet guilty about using it, angry at the loss of the cosy sanctuary of the womb and the privilege of childhood, have made their sex a claim to power and then used their power to claim control of sex. In fact and fantasy, they have violently segregated black men and white women. The most notorious fantasy claims that the black man is sexually evil, low, subhuman; the white woman sexually pure elevated, superhuman. Together they dramatize the polarities of excrement and disembodied spirituality. Blacks and women have been sexual victims, often cruelly so: the black

man castrated, the woman raped and often treated to a psychic clitoridectomy.

For Stimpson, black is black male and woman is white female, and though she is depicting the white male as racist, she conjures an image of white women and black men sharing oppression only to argue that they must go their separate ways, and in so doing she makes use of the sex/race analogy in such a way as to curry favor from racist white men. Ironically, she admonishes white women not to make analogies between blacks and themselves but she continues to do just that in her essay. By suggesting that without rights they are placed in the same category as black men, white women appeal to the anti-black-male racism of white patriarchal men. Their argument for "women's liberation" (which for them is synonymous with white women's liberation) thus becomes an appeal to white men to maintain the racial hierarchy that grants white women a higher social status than black men.

Whenever black women tried to express to white women their ideas about white female racism or their sense that the women who were at the forefront of the movement were not oppressed women they were told that "oppression cannot be measured." White female emphasis on "common oppression" in their appeals to black women to join the movement further alienated many black women. Because so many of the white women in the movement were employers of non-white and white domestics, their rhetoric of common oppression was experienced by black women as an assault, an expression of the bourgeois woman's insensitivity and lack of concern for the lower class woman's position in society.

Underlying the assertion of common oppression was a patronizing attitude toward black women. White women were assuming that all they had to do was express a desire for sisterhood, or a desire to have black women join their groups, and black women would be overjoyed. They saw themselves as acting in a generous, open, non-racist manner and were shocked that black women responded to their overtures with anger and outrage. They could not see that their generosity was directed at themselves, that it was self-centered and motivated by their own opportunistic desires.

Despite the reality that white upper and middle class women in America suffer from sexist discrimination and sexist abuse, they are not as a group as oppressed as *poor* white, or black, or yellow women. Their unwillingness to distinguish between various degrees of discrimination or oppression caused black women to see them as enemies. As many upper and middle class white feminists who suffer least from sexist oppression were attempting to focus all attention on themselves, it follows that they would not accept an analysis of woman's lot in America which argued that not all women are equally oppressed because some women are able to use their class, race, and educational privilege to effectively resist sexist oppression.

Initially, class privilege was not discussed by white women in the women's movement. They wanted to project an image of themselves as victims and that could not be done by drawing attention to their class. In fact, the contemporary women's movement was extremely class bound. As a group, white participants did not denounce capitalism. They chose to define liberation using the terms of white capitalist patriarchy, equating liberation with gaining economic status and money power. Like all good capitalists, they proclaimed work as the key to liberation. This emphasis on work was yet another indication of the extent to which the white female liberationists' perception of reality was totally narcissistic, classist, and racist. Implicit in the assertion that work was the key to women's liberation was a refusal to acknowledge the reality that, for masses of American working class women, working for pay neither liberated them from sexist oppression nor allowed them to gain any measure of economic independence. In *Liberating Feminism*, Benjamin Barber's critique of the women's movement, he comments on the white middle and upper class women's liberationist focus on work:

> Work clearly means something very different to women in search of an escape from leisure than it has to most of the human race for most of history. For a few lucky men, for far fewer women, work has occasionally been a source of meaning and creativity. But for most of the rest it remains even now forced drudgery in front of the ploughs, machines,

words or numbers—pushing products, pushing switches, pushing papers to eke out the wherewithal of material existence.

...To be able to work and to have work are two different matters. I suspect, however, that few liberationist women are to be found working as menials and unskilled laborers simply in order to occupy their time and identify with the power structure. For status and power are not conferred by work per se, but by certain kinds of work generally reserved to the middle and upper classes.... As Studs Terkel shows in *Working*, most workers find jobs dull, oppressive, frustrating and alienating—very much what women find housewifery.

When white women's liberationists emphasized work as a path to liberation, they did not concentrate their attention on those women who are most exploited in the American labor force. Had they emphasized the plight of working class women, attention would have shifted away from the college-educated suburban housewife who wanted entrance into the middle and upper class work force. Had attention been focused on women who were already working and who were exploited as cheap surplus labor in American society, it would have de-romanticized the middle class white woman's quest for "meaningful" employment. While it does not in any way diminish the importance of women resisting sexist oppression by entering the labor force, work has not been a liberating force for masses of American women. And for some time now, sexism has not prevented them from being in the work force. White middle and upper class women like those described in Betty Friedan's *The Feminine Mystique* were housewives not because sexism would have prevented them from being in the paid labor force, but because they had willingly embraced the notion that it was better to be a housewife than to be a worker. The racism and classism of white women's liberationists was most apparent whenever they discussed work as the liberating force for women. In such discussions it was always the middle class "housewife" who was depicted as the victim of sexist oppression and not the poor black and non-black women who are most exploited by American economics.

Throughout woman's history as a paid laborer, white

women workers have been able to enter the work force much later than black women yet advance at a much more rapid pace. Even though all women were denied access to many jobs because of sexist discrimination, racism ensured that the lot of the white women would always be better than that of the black female worker. Pauli Murray compared the status of the two groups in her essay "The Liberation of Black Women" and noted:

> When we compare the position of the black woman to that of the white woman, we find that she remains single more often, bears more children, is in the labor market longer and in greater proportion, has less education, earns less, is widowed earlier, and carries a relatively heavier economic responsibility as family head than her white counterpart.

Often in discussions of woman's status in the labor force, white women liberationists choose to ignore or minimize the disparity between the economic status of black women and that of white women. White activist Jo Freeman addresses the issue in *The Politics of Women's Liberation* when she comments that black women have the "highest unemployment rates and lowest median income of any race/sex group." But she then minimizes the impact of this assertion in a sentence that follows: "Of all race/sex groups of full-time workers, non-white women have had the greatest percentage increase in their median income since 1939, and white women have had the lowest." Freeman does not inform readers that the wages black women received were not a reflection of an advancing economic status so much as they were an indication that the wages paid them, for so long considerably lower than those paid white women, were approaching the set norm.

Few, if any, white women liberationists are willing to acknowledge that the women's movement was consciously and deliberately structured to exclude black and other non-white women and to serve primarily the interests of middle and upper class college-educated white women seeking social equality with middle and upper class white men. While they may agree that white women involved with women's liberationist groups are racist and classist they tend to feel that this in no way undermines the movement. But it is precisely the racism and classism of exponents of feminist ideology that has caused a large majority of black women to suspect their motives, and to reject active participation in any effort to organize a women's movement. Black woman activist Dorothy Bolden, who worked forty-two years as a maid in Atlanta, one of the founders of the National Domestic Workers, Inc., voiced her opinions of the movement in *Nobody Speaks for Me! Self Portraits of Working Class Women*:

> ... I was very proud to see them stand up and speak up when it started. I'm glad to see any group do that when they're righteous and I know they have been denied something. But they're not talking about the masses of people. You've got different classes of people in all phases of life and all races, and those people have to be spoken up for too.
> ... You can't talk about women's rights until we include all women. When you deny one woman of her rights, you deny all. I'm getting tired of going to those meetings, because there's none of us participating.
> They're still trying to put their amendment to the constitution, but they're not going to be able to do it until they include us. Some of these states know this, that you don't have all women up front supporting that amendment. They are talking about women's rights but which women?

It is often assumed that all black women are simply not interested in women's liberation. White women's liberationists have helped to perpetuate the belief that black women would rather remain in stereotypically female roles than have social equality with men. Yet a Louis Harris Virginia Slims poll conducted in 1972 revealed that sixty-two percent of black women supported efforts to change woman's status in society as compared to forty-five percent of white women, and that sixty-seven percent of black women were sympathetic to women's liberation groups compared with only thirty-five percent of white women. The findings of the Harris poll suggest it is not opposition to feminist ideology that has caused black women to reject involvement in the women's movement.

Feminism as a political ideology advocating social equality for all women was and is acceptable to many black women. They rejected the women's movement when it became apparent that middle and upper class college-educated white women who were its majority participants were determined to shape the movement so that it would serve their own opportunistic ends. While the established definition of feminism is the theory of the political, economic, and social equality of the sexes, white women liberationists used the power granted them by virtue of their being members of the dominant race in American society to interpret feminism in such a way that it was no longer relevant to all women. And it seemed incredible to black women that they were being asked to support a movement whose majority participants were eager to maintain race and class hierarchies between women.

Black women who participated in women's groups, lectures, and meetings initially trusted the sincerity of white female participants. Like 19th century black women's rights advocates, they assumed that any women's movement would address issues relevant to all women and that racism would be automatically cited as a force that had divided women, that would have to be reckoned with for true Sisterhood to emerge, and also that no radical revolutionary women's movement could take place until women as a group were joined in political solidarity. Although contemporary black women were mindful of the prevalence of white female racism, they believed it could be confronted and changed.

As they participated in the women's movement they found, in their dialogues with white women in women's groups, in women's studies classes, at conferences, that their trust was betrayed. They found that white women had appropriated feminism to advance their own cause, i.e., their desire to enter the mainstream of American capitalism. They were told that white women were in the majority and that they had the power to decide which issues would be considered "feminist" issues. White women liberationists decided that the way to confront racism was to speak out in consciousness-raising groups about their racist upbringings, to encourage black women to join their cause, to make sure they hired one non-white woman in "their" women's studies program, or to invite one non-white woman to speak on a discussion panel at "their" conference.

When black women involved with women's liberation

attempted to discuss racism, many white women responded by angrily stating: "We won't be guilt-tripped." For them the dialogue ceased. Others seemed to relish admitting that they were racist but felt that admitting verbally to being racist was tantamount to changing their racist values. For the most part, white women refused to listen when black women explained that what they expected was not verbal admissions of guilt but conscious gestures and acts that would show that white women liberationists were anti-racist and attempting to overcome their racism. The issue of racism within the women's movement would never have been raised had white women shown in their writings and speeches that they were in fact "liberated" from racism.

As concerned black and white individuals tried to stress the importance to the women's movement of confronting and changing racist attitudes because such sentiments threatened to undermine the movement, they met with resistance from those white women who saw feminism solely as a vehicle to enhance their own individual, opportunistic ends. Conservative, reactionary white women, who increasingly represented a large majority of the participants, were outspoken in their pronouncements that the issue of racism should not be considered worthy of attention. They did not want the issue of racism raised because they did not want to deflect attention away from their projection of the white woman as "good," i.e., non-racist victim, and the white man as "bad," i.e., racist oppressor. For them to have acknowledged woman's active complicity in the perpetuation of imperialism, colonialism, racism, or sexism would have made the issue of women's liberation far more complex. To those who saw feminism solely as a way to demand entrance into the white male power structure, it simplified matters to make all men oppressors and all women victims.

Some black women who were interested in women's liberation responded to the racism of white female participants by forming separate "black feminist" groups. This response was reactionary. By creating segregated feminist groups, they both endorsed and perpetuated the very "racism" they were supposedly attacking. They did not provide a critical evaluation of the women's movement and offer to all women a feminist ideology uncorrupted by racism or the opportunistic desires of individual groups. Instead, as colonized people have done for centuries, they accepted the terms imposed upon them by the dominant group (in this instance white women liberationists) and structured their groups on a racist platform identical to that of the white-dominated groups they were reacting against. White women were actively excluded from black groups. In fact, the distinguishing characteristic of the black "feminist" group was its focus on issues relating specifically to black women. The emphasis on black women was made public in the writings of black participants. The Combahee River Collective published "A Black Feminist Statement" to explain their group's focus. In their opening paragraph they declared:

> We are a collective of black feminists who have been meeting together since 1974. During that time we have been involved in the process of defining and clarifying our politics, while at the same time doing political work within our own group and in coalition with other progressive organizations and movements. The most general state-ment of our politics at the present time would be that we are actively committed to struggling against racial, sexual, heterosexual, and class oppression and see as our particular task the development of integrated analysis and practice based upon the fact that the major systems of oppression are interlocking. The synthesis of these oppressions creates the conditions of our lives. As black women we see black feminism as the logical political movement to combat the manifold and simultaneous oppression that all women of color face.

The emergence of black feminist groups led to a greater polarization of black and white women's liberationists. Instead of bonding on the basis of shared understanding of woman's varied collective and individual plight in society, they acted as if the distance separating their experiences from one another could not be bridged by knowledge or understanding. Rather than black women attacking the white female attempt to pre-sent them as an Other, an unknown, unfathomable element, they acted as if they were an Other. Many black women found an affirmation and support of their concern with feminism in all-black groups that they had not experienced in women's groups dominated by white women; this has been one of the positive features of black women's groups. However, all women should experience in racially mixed groups affirmation and support. Racism is the barrier that prevents positive communication and it is not eliminated or challenged by separation. White women supported the formation of separate groups because it confirmed their preconceived racist-sexist notion that no connection existed between their experiences and those of black women. Separate groups meant they would not be asked to concern themselves with race or racism. While black women condemned the anti-black racism of white women, the mounting animosity between the two groups gave rise to overt expression of their anti-white racism. Many black women who had never participated in the women's movement saw the formation of separate black groups as confirmation of their belief that no alliance could ever take place between black and white women. To express their anger and rage at white women, they evoked the negative stereotypical image of the white woman as a passive, parasitic, privileged being living off the labor of others as a way to mock and ridicule the white women liberationists. Black woman Lorraine Bethel published a poem entitled "What Chou Mean We, White Girl? Or. The Cullud Lesbian Feminist Declaration of Independence" prefaced with the statement:

> I bought a sweater at a yard sale from a white-skinned (as opposed to Anglo-Saxon) woman. When wearing it I am struck by the smell—it reeks of a soft, privileged life without stress, sweat, or struggle. When wearing it I often think to myself, this sweater smells of a comfort, a way of being in the world I have never known in my life, and never will. It's the same feeling I experience walking through Bonwit Teller's and seeing white-skinned women buying trinkets that cost enough to support the elderly Black Woman elevator operator, who stands on her feet all day taking them up and down, for the rest of her life. It is moments/ infinities of conscious pain like these that make me want to cry/kill/roll my eyes suck my teeth hand on my hip scream at so-called radical white lesbians/feminist(s) "WHAT CHOU MEAN WE, WHITE GIRL?"

Animosity between black and white women's liberationists was not due solely to disagreement over racism within the
women's movement; it was the end result of years of jealousy,
envy, competition, and anger between the two groups. Conflict
between black and white women did not begin with the 20th
century women's movement. It began during slavery. The social
status of white women in America has to a large extent been
determined by white people's relationship to black people. It
was the enslavement of African people in colonized America
that marked the beginning of a change in the social status of
white women. Prior to slavery, patriarchal law decreed white
women were lowly inferior beings, the subordinate group in
society. The subjugation of black people allowed them to vacate
their despised position and assume the role of a superior.

Consequently, it can be easily argued that even though
white men institutionalized slavery, white women were its
most immediate beneficiaries. Slavery in no way altered the
hierarchical social status of the white male but it created a new
status for the white female. The only way that her new status
could be maintained was through the constant assertion of her
superiority over the black woman and man. All too often
colonial white women, particularly those who were slave
mistresses, chose to differentiate their status from the slave's
by treating the slave in a brutal and cruel manner. It was in her
relationship to the black female slave that the white woman
could best assert her power. Individual black slave women were
quick to learn that sex-role differentiation did not mean that
the white mistress was not to be regarded as an authority figure.
Because they had been socialized via patriarchy to respect male
authority and resent female authority, black women were
reluctant to acknowledge the "power" of the white mistress.
When the enslaved black woman expressed contempt and
disregard for white female authority, the white mistress often
resorted to brutal punishment to assert her authority. But even
brutal punishment could not change the fact that black women
were not inclined to regard the white female with the awe and
respect they showed to the white male.

By flaunting their sexual lust for the bodies of black
women and their preference for them as sexual partners, white

men successfully pitted white women and enslaved black women against one another. In most instances, the white mistress did not envy the black female slave her role as sexual object; she feared only that her newly acquired social status might be threatened by white male sexual interaction with black women. His sexual involvement with black women (even if that involvement was rape) in effect reminded the white female of her subordinate position in relationship to him. For he could exercise his power as racial imperialist and sexual imperialist to rape or seduce black women, while white women were not free to rape or seduce black men without fear of punishment. Though the white female might condemn the actions of a white male who chose to interact sexually with black female slaves, she was unable to dictate to him proper behavior. Nor could she retaliate by engaging in sexual relationships with enslaved or free black men. Not surprisingly, she directed her anger and rage at the enslaved black women. In those cases where emotional ties developed between white men and black female slaves, white mistresses would go to great lengths to punish the female. Severe beatings were the method most white women used to punish black female slaves. Often in a jealous rage a mistress might use disfigurement to punish a lusted-after black female slave. The mistress might cut off her breast, blind an eye, or cut off another body part. Such treatment naturally caused hostility between white women and enslaved black women. To the enslaved black woman, the white mistress living in relative comfort was the representative symbol of white womanhood. She was both envied and despised—envied for her material comfort, despised because she felt little concern or compassion for the slave woman's lot. Since the white woman's privileged social status could only exist if a group of women were present to assume the lowly position she had abdicated, it follows that black and white women would be at odds with one another. If the white woman struggled to change the lot of the black slave woman, her own social position on the race-sex hierarchy would be altered.

Manumission did not bring an end to conflicts between black and white women; it heightened them. To maintain the apartheid structure slavery had institutionalized, white colonizers, male and female, created a variety of myths and stereotypes to differentiate the status of black women from that of white women. White racists and even some black people who had absorbed the colonizer's mentality depicted the white woman as a symbol of perfect womanhood and encouraged black women to strive to attain such perfection by using the white female as her model. The jealousy and envy of white women that had erupted in the black woman's consciousness during slavery was deliberately encouraged by the dominant white culture. Advertisements, newspaper articles, books, etc., were constant reminders to black women of the difference between their social status and that of white women, and they bitterly resented it. Nowhere was this dichotomy as clearly demonstrated as in the materially privileged white household where the black female domestic worked as an employee of the white family. In these relationships, black women workers were exploited to enhance the social standing of white families. In the white community, employing domestic help was a sign of material privilege and the person who directly benefited from a servant's work was the white woman, since without the servant she would have performed domestic chores. Not surprisingly, the black female domestic tended to see the white female as her "boss," her oppressor, not the white male whose earnings usually paid her wage.

Throughout American history white men have deliberately promoted hostility and divisiveness between white and black women. The white patriarchal power structure pits the two groups against each other, preventing the growth of solidarity between women and ensuring that woman's status as a subordinate group under patriarchy remains intact. To this end, white men have supported changes in the white woman's social standing only if there exists another female group to assume that role. Consequently, the white patriarch undergoes no radical change in his sexist assumption that woman is inherently inferior. He neither relinquishes his dominant position nor alters the patriarchal structure of society. He is, however, able to convince many white women that fundamental changes in "woman's status" have occurred because he has successfully socialized her, via racism, to assume that no connection exists between her and black women.

Because women's liberation has been equated with gaining privileges within the white male power structure, white men—and not women, either white or black—have dictated the terms by which women are allowed entrance into the system. One of the terms male patriarchs have set is that one group of women is granted privileges that they obtain by actively supporting the oppression and exploitation of other groups of women. White and black women have been socialized to accept and honor these terms, hence the fierce competition between the two groups; a competition that has always been centered in the arena of sexual politics, with white and black women competing against one another for male favor. This competition is part of an overall battle between various groups of women to be the chosen female group.

The contemporary move toward feminist revolution was continually undermined by competition between various factions. In regards to race, the women's movement has become simply another arena in which white and black women compete to be the chosen female group. This power struggle has not been resolved by the formation of opposing interest groups. Such groups are symptomatic of the problem and are no solution. Black and white women have for so long allowed their idea of liberation to be formed by the existing status quo that they have not yet devised a strategy by which we can come together. They have had only a slave's idea of freedom. And to the slave, the master's way of life represents the ideal free lifestyle.

Women's liberationists, white and black, will always be at odds with one another as long as our idea of liberation is based on having the power white men have. For that power denies unity, denies common connections, and is inherently divisive. It is woman's acceptance of divisiveness as a natural order that has caused black and white women to cling religiously to the belief that bonding across racial boundaries is impossible, to passively accept the notion that the distances that separate women are immutable. Even though the most uninformed and naive women's liberationist knows that Sisterhood as political bonding between women is necessary for feminist revolution, women have not struggled long or hard enough to overcome the societal brainwashing that has impressed on our psyches the belief that no union between black and white women can ever be forged. The methods women have employed to reach one another across racial boundaries have been shallow, superficial, and destined to fail.

Resolution of the conflict between black and white women cannot begin until all women acknowledge that a feminist movement which is both racist and classist is a mere sham, a cover-up for women's continued bondage to materialist patriarchal principles, and passive acceptance of the status quo. The sisterhood that is necessary for the making of feminist revolution can be achieved only when all women disengage themselves from the hostility, jealousy, and competition with one another that has kept us vulnerable, weak, and unable to envision new realities. That sisterhood cannot be forged by the mere saying of words. It is the outcome of continued growth and change. It is a goal to be reached, a process of becoming. The process begins with action, with the individual woman's refusal to accept any set of myths, stereotypes, and false assumptions that deny the shared commonness of her human experience; that deny her capacity to experience the Unity of all life; that deny her capacity to bridge gaps created by racism, sexism, or classism; that deny her ability to change. The process begins with the individual woman's acceptance that American women, without exception, are socialized to be racist, classist, and sexist, in varying degrees, and that labeling ourselves feminists does not change the fact that we must consciously work to rid ourselves of the legacy of negative socialization.

If women want a feminist revolution—ours is a world that is crying out for feminist revolution—then we must assume responsibility for drawing women together in political solidarity. That means we must assume responsibility for eliminating all the forces that divide women. Racism is one such force. Women, all women, are accountable for racism continuing to divide us. Our willingness to assume responsibility for the elimination of racism need not be engendered by feelings of guilt, moral responsibility, victimization, or rage. It can spring from a heartfelt desire for sisterhood and the personal, intellectual realization that racism among women undermines the potential radicalism of feminism. It can spring from our knowledge that racism is an obstacle in our path that must be removed. More obstacles are created if we simply engage in endless debate as to who put it there.

Black Women and Feminism

More than a hundred years have passed since the day Sojourner Truth stood before an assembled body of white women and men at an anti-slavery rally in Indiana and bared her breasts to prove that she was indeed a woman. To Sojourner, who had traveled the long road from slavery to freedom, the baring of her breasts was a small matter. She faced her audience without fear, without shame, proud of having been born black and female. Yet the white man who yelled at Sojourner, "I don't believe you really are a woman," unwittingly voiced America's contempt and disrespect for black womanhood. In the eyes of the 19th century white public, the black female was a creature unworthy of the title woman; she was mere chattel, a thing, an animal. When Sojourner Truth stood before the second annual convention of the women's rights movement in Akron, Ohio, in 1852, white women who deemed it unfitting that a black woman should speak on a public platform in their presence screamed: "Don't let her speak! Don't let her speak! Don't let her speak!" Sojourner endured their protests and became one of the first feminists to call their attention to the lot of the black slave woman who, compelled by circumstance to labor alongside black men, was a living embodiment of the truth that women could be the work-equals of men.

It was no mere coincidence that Sojourner Truth was allowed on stage after a white male spoke against the idea of equal rights for women, basing his argument on the notion that woman was too weak to perform her share of manual labor— that she was innately the physical inferior to man. Sojourner quickly responded to his argument, telling her audience:

> ...Well, children, whar dar is so much racket dar must be something out o' kilter. I tink dat 'twixt de niggers of de Souf and de women at de Norf all a talkin 'bout rights, de white men will be in a fix pretty soon. But what's all dis here talkin' 'bout? Dat man ober dar say dat women needs to be helped into carriages, and lifted ober ditches, and to have de best places... and ain't I a woman? Look at me! Look at my arm!... I have plowed, and planted, and gathered into barns, and no man could head me—and ain't I a woman? I could work as much as any man (when I could get it), and bear de lash as well—and ain't I a woman? I have borne five children and I seen 'em mos all sold off into slavery, and when I cried out with a mother's grief, none but Jesus hear—and ain't I a woman?

Unlike most white women's rights advocates, Sojourner Truth could refer to her own personal life experience as evidence of woman's ability to function as a parent; to be the work equal of man; to undergo persecution, physical abuse, rape, torture; and to not only survive but emerge triumphant.

Sojourner Truth was not the only black woman to advocate social equality for women. Her eagerness to speak publicly in favor of women's rights despite public disapproval and resistance paved the way for other politically-minded black women to express their views. Sexism and racism have so informed the perspective of American historiographers that they have tended to overlook and exclude the effort of black women in discussions of the American women's rights movement. White female scholars who support feminist ideology have also ignored the contribution of black women. In contemporary works, like *The Remembered Gate: Origins of American Feminism* by Barbara Berg, *Herstory* by June Sochen, *Hidden from History* by Sheila Rowbothan, *The Women's Movement* by Barbara Deckard, to name a few, the role black women played as advocates for women's rights in the 19th century is never mentioned. Eleanor Flexner's *Century of Struggle*, which was first published in 1959, remains one of the very few book-length historical works on the women's rights movement that documents the participation of black women.

Most women involved in the recent move toward a feminist revolution assume that white women have initiated all feminist resistance to male chauvinism in American society, and further assume that black women are not interested in women's liberation. While it is true that white women have led every movement toward feminist revolution in American society, their dominance is less a sign of black female disinterest in feminist struggle than an indication that the politics of colonization and racial imperialism have made it historically impossible for black women in the United States to lead a women's movement.

Nineteenth century black women were more aware of sexist oppression than any other female group in American society has ever been. Not only were they the female group most victimized by sexist discrimination and sexist oppression, their powerlessness was such that resistance on their part could rarely take the form of organized collective action. The 19th century women's rights movement could have provided a forum for black women to address their grievances, but white female racism barred them from full participation in the movement. Furthermore, it served as a grave reminder that racism had to be eliminated before black women would be recognized as having an equal voice with white women on the issue of women's rights. Women's organizations and clubs in the 19th century were almost always racially segregated, but that did not mean that black female participants in such groups were any less committed to women's rights than white participants.

Contemporary historiographers tend to over-emphasize the 19th century black female's commitment to eliminating racism so as to make it seem that their involvement with anti-racist work precluded involvement in women's rights activities. An example of this trend can be found in June Sochen's work *Herstory*, where she discusses white women's organizations in a chapter titled "The Women's Movement" but discusses black women's organizations in a chapter titled "Old Problems: Black Americans," a categorization which implies that black women's organizations emerged as part of the general effort of black people to end racism, not as part of their participation in the women's movement. Sochen writes:

> Black women's clubs were organized locally to perform charitable and educational services. Similar in purpose and nature to white women's clubs, the National Association of Colored Women was formed in 1896 and, led by Mary Church Terrell (1863-1954), it had more than 100,000 members in 26 states within four years. While one local chapter would be organizing a hospital for blacks, another would be developing a kindergarten program for the black children of its community.
>
> One of the first black women to graduate from Oberlin College, Mary Church Terrell was an articulate and prominent spokeswoman for black Americans' rights. An extraordinary person, she spent her long life working for the freedom of black people. She was a good speaker and writer for a variety of causes. In addition to heading the NACW, Mrs. Terrell campaigned against lynching, became a charter member of the NAACP, and worked for the suffrage movement as well. She represented black women at many national and international meetings.

From the information provided in these paragraphs, readers might easily conclude that Mary Church Terrell was a passionate spokesperson for black American rights who was not overly concerned with rights for women. This was not so. As president of the National Association of Colored Women, Mary Church Terrell worked arduously to involve black women in the women's rights struggle. She was particularly concerned that they struggle to obtain social equality for their sex in the educational sphere. That Mary Church Terrell, like most black women's rights advocates, was also committed to uplifting her race as a whole in no way diminished the fact that the focus of her attention was on changing the role of women in society. Had Terrell considered herself to be a spokesperson for the black race as a whole she would not have published "A Colored Woman in a White World," a narrative that discussed the social status of black women and the impact of racism and sexism on their lives.

No white feminist historian would write about the efforts of Lucy Stone, Elizabeth Stanton, Lucretia Mott and others to initiate social reforms that would affect primarily white women as if their efforts were completely divorced from the issue of women's rights. Yet historians who label themselves feminist continually minimize the contribution of black women's rights advocates by implying that their focus was solely on racial reform measures. Because of white racial imperialism, white women could organize groups like the Women's Christian Temperance Union, Young Women's Christian Association, General Federation of Women's Clubs, without explicitly stating in their heading that these organizations were exclusively white. Black women identified themselves racially calling their groups Colored Women's League, National Federation of Afro-American Women, National Association for Colored Women, and because they identified themselves by race scholars assume that their interest in the elevation of blacks as a group overshadowed their involvement with woman's effort to effect social reform. In fact, black female reform organizations were solidly rooted in the women's movement. It was in reaction to the racism of white women and to the fact that the U.S. remained a society with an apartheid social structure that compelled black women to focus on themselves rather than all women.

Black activist Josephine St. Pierre Ruffin tried to work with white women's organizations and found that black women could not depend on racist white women to encourage them to fully participate in the women's reform movement; consequently, she demanded that black women organize to address issues for themselves. At the First National Conference of Colored Women held in Boston in 1895, she told her audience:

> The reasons why we should confer are so apparent that it would seem hardly necessary to enumerate them, and yet there is none of them but demand our serious consideration. In the first place we need to feel the cheer and

inspiration of meeting with each other, we need to gain the courage and fresh life that comes from the mingling of congenial souls, of those working for the same ends. Next, we need to talk over not only those things which are of vital importance to us as women, but also the things that are of especial interest to us as colored women, the training of our children, openings for our boys and girls how they can be prepared for occupations and occupations may be found or opened for them, what we especially can do in the moral education of the race with which we are identified, our mental elevation and physical development, the home training it is necessary to give our children in order to prepare them to meet the peculiar conditions in which they shall find themselves, how to make the most of our own, to some extent limited opportunities, these are some of our own peculiar questions to be discussed. Besides these are the general questions of the day, which we cannot afford to be indifferent to....

Ruffin did not encourage black women's rights advocates to work solely to improve their own lot, she maintained that black women needed to organize so that they could lead a women's movement that would address the concerns of all women:

Our woman's movement is a woman's movement that is led and directed by women for the good of women and men, for the benefit of all humanity, which is more than any one branch or section of it. We want, we ask the active interest of our men, and, too, we are not drawing the color line; we are women, American women, as intensely interested in all that pertains to us as such as all other American women; we are not alienating or withdrawing, we are only coming to the front, willing to join any others in the same work and cordially inviting and welcoming any others to join us.

Other black women's rights advocates echoed Ruffin's sentiments. Despite the fact that white racial imperialism excluded black women from participating in groups with white women, they remained committed to the belief that women's rights could be attained only if women joined together to present a united front. Addressing the World Congress of Representative Women, black suffragist Fannie Barrier Williams made it known that black women were as committed to the struggle for women's rights as any other group of women. In her address she voiced the belief that women joined in political solidarity would have a tremendous impact on American culture:

> The power of organized womanhood is one of the most interesting studies of modern sociology. Formerly women knew so little of each other mentally, their common interests were so sentimental and gossipy, and their knowledge of all the larger affairs of human society was so meager that organization among them, in the modern sense, was impossible. Now their liberal intelligence, their contact in all the great interest of education, and their increasing influence for good in all the great reformatory movements of the age has created in them a greater respect for each other, and furnished the elements of organization for large and splendid purposes. The highest ascendancy of woman's development has been reached when they have become mentally strong enough to find bonds of association interwoven with sympathy, loyalty, and mutual trustfulness. To-day union is the watchword of woman's onward march.

Although racial segregation was the norm in women's organizations, reform measures initiated by white and black women's groups were not radically different. They differed only in that black women included in their reform efforts measures that were aimed at solving specific problems they faced. One such problem was the general tendency among white Americans and even some brainwashed blacks to regard all black women as sexually immoral, licentious, and wanton—a negative stereotype that had its origin in American sexist mythology. Consequently, while white women's organizations could concentrate their attentions on general reform measures, black women had to launch a campaign to defend their "virtue." As part of their campaign they wrote articles and speeches upholding black female sexual morality.

White women's organizations could confine their attention to issues such as education, charity, or to the formation of literary societies, while black women were concerned with issues such as poverty, care for the elderly and disabled, or prostitution. Black female clubs and organizations were potentially more feminist and radical in nature than white women's clubs because of the difference in their circumstance created by racist oppression. White women as a group did not have to launch an attack on prostitution as did black women. Many young black women leaving the South and migrating north were compelled to work as prostitutes. In some cases, they would come north on what was called a Justice ticket, supplied them by employment agencies or labor agents. In exchange for transportation and the guarantee of a job on arrival, black women signed contracts to work where the agent placed them and agreed to pay a fee equivalent to one or two months' wages. On arriving north they would find their jobs were mainly as maids in houses of prostitution. Unable to survive on the low salary paid them, they would be encouraged to become prostitutes by white "pimps." The National League for the Protection of Colored Women was formed to inform and aid southern black women migrating north. In 1897, black activist Victoria Earle Matthews formed the White Rose Working Girl's Home and a Black Protection and Women's Rights Society in the Women's Loyal Union of New York and Brooklyn. To further acquaint the public with the plight of white women, Victoria Matthews delivered a lecture on "The Awakening of the Afro-American Woman." Her work was not done in isolation. Numerous black women's organizations were formed to help black women in their struggle for self-improvement.

Of those black women who advocated social equality for women, Anna Julia Cooper was one of the most outstanding. She was one of the first black activists to urge black women to articulate their own experiences and to make the public aware of the way in which racism and sexism together affected their social status. Ann Cooper wrote:

> The colored woman of today occupies, one might say, a unique position in this country. In a period of itself transitional and unsettled, her status seems one of the ascertainable and definitive of all the forces which makes for our civilization. She is confronted by a woman question and a race problem, and is as yet an unknown or unacknowledged factor in both.

Anna Cooper wanted the U.S. public to recognize the role black women played not just as spokespersons for their race but as advocates of rights for women. To spread her views on women's rights, she published *A Voice from the South* in 1892, one of the first feminist discussions of the social status of black women and a lengthy discussion of woman's right to higher education. In *A Voice from the South*, Cooper reiterated her belief that black women should not assume a passive subordinate position in relationship to black men. She also criticized black males for their refusal to support woman's effort to obtain equal rights. Since it was common for black leaders to question whether or not black female involvement in the struggle for women's rights would undermine their involvement in the struggle to eliminate racism, Cooper maintained that social equality of the sexes would mean that black women would be able to serve as leaders in the struggle against racism. She further argued that they had in fact shown themselves to be as committed to the black liberation struggle as black men, if not more so.

Included in *A Voice from the South* was an essay by Cooper on "The Higher Education of Women" in which she argued that women as a collective group should have the right to acquire higher education. Like many modern-day feminists, Cooper believed in the existence of a distinct "feminine principle" and argued that "a great want of the world in the past has been a feminine force," a force which could have "its full effect only through the untrammelled development of women."

> All I claim is that there is a feminine as well as a masculine side to truth; that these are related not as inferior and superior, not as better and worse, not as weaker and stronger, but as complements—complements in one necessary and symmetric whole. That as the man is more noble in reason, so the woman is more quick in sympathy. That as he is indefatigable in pursuit of abstract truth, so is she in caring for the interests by the way— striving tenderly and lovingly that not one of the least of these "little ones" should perish. That while we not unfrequently see women who reason, we say, with the coolness and precision of a man, and men as considerate of helplessness as a woman, still there is a general consensus of mankind that one trait is essentially masculine and the

> other is peculiarly feminine. That both are needed to be worked into the training of children, in order that boys may supplement their virility by tenderness and sensibility, and our girls may round out their gentleness by strength and self-reliance. That, as both are alike necessary in giving symmetry to the individual, so a nation or a race will degenerate into mere emotionalism on the one hand, or bullying on the other, if dominated by either exclusively; lastly, and most emphatically, that the feminine factor can have its proper effect only through woman's development and education so that she may fitly and intelligently stamp her force on the forces of her day, and add her modicum to the riches of the world's thought....

Even though Anna Cooper, like other 19th century women's rights advocates, continued to believe that woman could best serve her country by using education to enhance the sex role assigned her by patriarchy, she was aware that higher education would also enable women to explore worlds outside the traditional realm of home and family. To answer those who argued that higher education interfered with marriage, Cooper replied:

> I grant you that intellectual development, with the self-reliance and capacity for earning a livelihood which it gives, renders woman less dependent on the marriage relation for physical support (which, by the way, does not always accompany it). Neither is she compelled to look to sexual love as the one sensation capable of giving tone and relish, movement and vim to the life she lives. Her horizon is extended. Her sympathies are broadened and deepened and multiplied. She is in closer touch with nature....

Nineteenth century black women believed that were they given the right to vote, they could change the educational system so that women would have the right to pursue fully their educational goals. To achieve this end they wholeheartedly supported woman suffrage. Black woman activist Frances Ellen Watkins Harper was more outspoken on the subject of woman suffrage than any other black woman of her day. In 1888 she addressed the International Council of Women in Washington and spoke on the importance of suffrage to black and white women. At the Columbian Exposition in Chicago in 1893 she delivered an address titled "Woman's Political Future" expressing her views on suffrage:

> I do not believe in unrestricted and universal suffrage for either men or women. I believe in moral and educational tests. I do not believe that the most ignorant and brutal man is better prepared to add value to the strength and durability of the government than the most cultured, upright, and intelligent woman.... The ballot in the hands of woman means power added to influence. How well she will use that power I can not foretell. Great evils stare us in the face that need to be throttled by the combined power of an upright manhood and an enlightened womanhood; and I know that no nation can gain its full measure of enlightenment and happiness if one-half of it is free and the other half is fettered. China compressed the feet of her women and thereby retarded the steps of her men.

Mary Church Terrell was yet another black female activist who lobbied in support of woman suffrage. In 1912, she addressed the National America Woman's Suffrage Association, of which she was a member on two occasions, speaking in support of woman suffrage. Terrell was also active in the movement to stop the lynching of black people. Her article "Lynching from a Negro's Point of View" was published in the 1904 issue of the *North American Review*, and it was in this essay that she first appealed to white women to involve themselves in the anti-lynching crusade. Terrell believed that white women acted as the accomplices of white men at lynchings, and she placed a measure of the responsibility for racism and racial oppression on their shoulders:

> Lynching is the aftermath of slavery. The white men who shoot negroes to death and flay them alive, and the white women who apply flaming torches to their oil-soaked bodies today, are the sons and daughters of women who had but little, if any, compassion on the race when it was enslaved. The men who lynch negroes to-day are, as a rule, the children of women who sat by their firesides happy and proud in the possession and affection of their own children, while they looked with unpitying eye and adamantine heart upon the anguish of slave mothers whose children had been sold away, when not overtken by a sadder fate.... It is too much to expect perhaps, that the

> children of women who for generations looked upon the
> hardships and the degradation of their sisters of a darker
> hue with few if any protests, should have mercy and com-
> passion upon the children of that oppressed race now. But
> what a tremendous influence for law and order, and what a
> mighty foe to mob violence Southern white women might
> be, if they would arise in the purity and power of their
> womanhood to implore their fathers, husbands and sons
> no longer to stain their hands with the black man's blood!...

Terrell's appeal to white women to bond with black women on
the basis of shared womanhood was a reiteration of the
sentiments of many 19th century black women who were
convinced that women could be a new political force in the U.S.

Despite racist and sexist oppression, the latter part of the
19th century was an important era in black woman's history.
Frances Ellen Watkins Harper was gloriously right when she
exclaimed, "If the fifteenth century discovered America to the
Old World, the nineteenth is discovering woman to herself."
The fervor over women's rights generated in the 19th century
continued in the 20th century and culminated in the ratifiction
of the Nineteenth Amendment in August 1920 which granted
all women the right to vote. In their struggle to win the vote,
black women had learned a bitter lesson. They found as they
worked for suffrage that many whites saw granting women the
right to vote as yet another way to maintain the oppressive
system of white racial imperialism. Southern white suffragists
rallied around a platform that argued that woman suffrage in
the South would strengthen white supremacy. Even though
woman suffrage would also grant black women the right to
vote, in the south white women outnumbered them by two to
one. In *The Emancipation of the American Woman*, Andrew
Sinclair discusses the racial politics of white women suffragists
and concludes:

> The undisguised racism of the Southern suffragists
> such as Kate Gordon and Laura Clay—two of the most
> powerful officers in the National American Association
> after Anthony's retirement—worried the suffragists from
> the North and the West. Although Carrie Catt and Anna
> Shaw had to be diplomatic to gain some Southern support
> for suffrage, they lost the crusading spirit of the old

abolitionists.... The vocabulary of the movement changed from the language of human rights to that of expediency. Negro women in the North were excluded from some suffrage parades, for fear of offending the South. As one Negro leader wrote to another about the suffragists, "All of them are mortally afraid of the South and if they could get the Suffrage Amendment through without enfranchising coloured women, they would do it in a moment."

The language of the Northern suffrage leaders, even that of Elizabeth Stanton, increasingly shifted towards the expedient of educated suffrage for women.... The promise of the American Revolution in terms of human equality and liberty was forgotten in an effort to win the vote for a limited number of white, Anglo-Saxon women, in the same way that the terms of the Constitution had once denied the principles of the Declaration of Independence.

As in the 19th century struggle over the issue of woman suffrage, in the 20th century struggle, race and sex became interlocking issues. Like their predecessors, white women consciously and deliberately supported white racial imperialism, openly disavowing feelings of empathy and political solidarity with black people. In their efforts to secure the ballot, white women's rights advocates willingly betrayed the feminist belief that voting was the natural right of every woman. Their willingness to compromise feminist principles allowed the patriarchal power structure to co-opt the energy of women suffragists and use the votes of women to strengthen the existing anti-woman political structure. The great majority of white women did not use their voting privileges to support women's issues; they voted as their husbands, fathers, or brothers voted. The more militant white suffragists had hoped that women would use the vote to form their own party rather than supporting major parties that denied women social equality with men. Voting privileges for women changed in no fundamental way the lot of women in society, but they did enable women to help support and maintain the existing white racist imperialist patriarchal social order. To a very grave extent women obtaining the right to vote was more a victory for racist principles than a triumph of feminist principles.

Black female suffragists found that the vote had little impact on their social status. The most militant wing of the

1920s women's movement, the National Woman's Party, was both racist and classist. Even though the party pledged to work for full equality for women, it actively worked to promote solely the interests of white middle and upper class women. In *Herstory,* June Sochen makes this comment on the attitude of white suffragists toward black women:

> After the woman's suffrage amendment was passed in 1920, some reformers wondered whether it would benefit black women as well as white women—especially in the South where black men had been virtually disenfranchised by the white power-holders. Over two million newly enfranchised black women lived in the South. When suffragists suggested to Alice Paul that the voting rights of black women would be a continuing vital issue, she replied that the year 1920 was not the time to discuss that question. Rather, she said, the suffragists should enjoy their new political power and make plans for other battles in the future. Yet as the reformers had foreseen, when black women went to the polls in Alabama or Georgia, they found that white election officials had a bag of tricks ready to prevent them from voting. If a black woman could read a complicated text put before her, the white official would find some other obscure reason why she was ineligible to vote. And any woman who persisted was threatened with violence if she did not obediently slink away.

When women suffrage failed to alter in any way the social status of black women, many black female suffragists became disillusioned with women's rights. They had supported woman suffrage only to find their interests betrayed, only to find that "woman suffrage" would be used as a weapon to strengthen white oppression of black people. They found that obtaining rights for women would have little impact on their social status as long as white racial imperialism automatically denied them full citizenship. While white women were rejoicing over obtaining the right to vote, a system of racial apartheid was being institutionalized throughout the U.S. that would threaten the freedom of black women far more crucially than sexual imperialism. That system of racial apartheid was called Jim Crow. In *The Strange Career of Jim Crow,* C. Vann Woodward describes this resurgence of racism:

In the postwar era there were new indications that the Southern Way was spreading as the American Way in race relations. The great migration of the Negro into the residential slum areas and the industrial plants of the big northern cities increased tension between races. Northern labor was jealous of its status and resentful of the competition of Negroes, who were excluded from unions. Negroes were pushed out of the more desirable jobs in industries that they had succeeded in invading during the manpower shortage of the war years. They were squeezed out of federal employment more and more. Negro postmen began to disappear from their old routes as they did from the police beats. They began to lose their grip upon crafts such as that of the barbers, which had once been a virtual monopoly in the South.

Racism in regimented form was spread over the whole country in the 'twenties by the new Ku Klux Klan....

There was no apparent tendency toward abatement or relaxation of the Jim Crow code of discrimination and segregation in the 1920's, and none in the 'thirties until well along in the depression years. In fact the Jim Crow laws were elaborated and further expanded in those years. Much social and economic history is reflected in the new laws. When women began to bob their hair and became patrons of the barber shops, Atlanta passed an ordinance in 1926 forbidding Negro barbers to serve women or children under fourteen years of age. Jim Crow kept step with the march of progress in transportation and industry, as well as with the changes in fashion.

As Jim Crow apartheid threatened to strip black people of the rights and achievements they had acquired during Reconstruction, it was only natural that black female activists ceased to struggle over women's rights issues and concentrated their energies on resisting racism.

Black women activists were not the only group of women to shift their attention away from women's rights issues. Because much of the energy of female activists had focused on the vote, once it was obtained many women saw no further need for a women's movement. Although white women in the Woman's Party continued feminist struggle, black women were rarely active participants. Their energies were focused on resisting mounting racial oppression. While white women's rights advocates struggled in 1933 to get the Senate to pass the Equal Rights Amendment, black women activists were fighting to prevent the lynching of black women and men by mobs of white racists, to improve the conditions of masses of poverty-stricken black people, and to provide educational opportunities. In the 20s and 30s, black female activists appealed to the masses of black women not to let sexism prevent them from being as involved as black men in the struggle to free black people. Amy Jacques Garvey, active in the black nationalist movement led by her co-worker and husband Marcus Garvey, edited the woman's page in *Negro World*, the newspaper publication of the Universal Negro Improvement Association. In her articles she urged black women to focus their attention on black national-ism and participate equally in the black liberation struggle.

> The exigencies of this present age require that women take their places beside their men. White women are rallying all their forces and united regardless of national boundaries to save their race from destruction, and preserve its ideals for posterity.... White men have begun to realize that as women are the backbone of the home, so can they, by their economic experience and their aptitude for details partici-pate effectively in guiding the destiny of nation and race.
>
> No line of endeavor remains closed for long to the modern woman. She agitates for equal opportunities and gets them; she makes good on the job and gains the respect of men who heretofore opposed her. She prefers to be a bread-winner than a half-starved wife at home. She is not afraid of hard work and by being independent she gets more out of the present-day husband than her grand-mother did in the good old days.
>
> The women of the East, both yellow and black, are slowly, but surely imitating the women of the Western world, and as the white women are bolstering up a decaying white civilization, even so women of the darker races are sallying forth to help their men establish a civilization according to their own standards, and to strive for world leadership.

Even though black women leaders urged black women to assume as active a role as black men in the struggle to end racism, underlying their call for action was the assumption that social equality of the sexes was a secondary consideration.

From the beginning of the women's rights movement, its staunch supporters had argued that social equality for women was a necessary step for patriotic nation-building. They stressed that women were not opposing the U.S. political or social order, but simply wanted to actively support the existing system of government. This attitude always threatened the occasional political solidarity that existed between black and white women's rights activists. To white women, full participation in the growth of the U.S. as a nation often included acceptance and support of white racial imperialism, while black women, even those who were most politically conservative, were often obliged to denounce the nation because of its racist policies. Eventually both groups of women allowed racial alliances to supersede feminist struggle. Racial segregation remained the norm in most women's organizations and clubs in the 30s and 40s. From 1940 to 1960, most women's groups did not emphasize women's liberation; women bonded together for social or professional reasons. Barbara Deckard, author of *The Women's Movement*, contends that there was no organized women's liberation movement from 1940 to 1960 and gave as an explanation these reasons:

> One reason was the limited ideology and elite class base of the suffragists. So strongly had they emphasized the vote, and only the vote, that their successors—like the League of Women Voters—could declare in the 1920's that there was no more discrimination against women and that liberal women should merely fight for general reforms for all people. The sole successor to the most militant suffragists —the Women's Party—was narrow in other ways. It continued to fight for equal legal rights but paid little or no attention to women's inferior position in the family, to the exploitation of women workers, or to the special problems of black women. This lack of interest in the major social, economic, and racial issues alienated radical women, while the hostile social atmosphere prevented them from winning over the moderate women.
>
>   By the mid-1920's, the relative stability of capitalism, the disappearance of the small radical farmer, the red-baiting and the internal splits, destroyed the Socialist and Progressive parties and brought a period of conservatism hostile to the women's movement. The radicalism of the

1930's concentrated on unemployment and, in the late 1930's, on the threat of war with fascism to the practical exclusion of all other issues. Again, during the war other issues could not be raised. The postwar 1946-1960 period was a time of U.S. economic expansion and world dominance, of the cold war and super-patriotism ensured by the witch hunting of McCarthyism. All radical and liberal groups suffered repression: and possible women's liberation causes—such as child care—were smothered with the rest.

In the forty years from the mid-1920s to the mid-1960s black female leaders no longer advocated women's rights. The struggle for black liberation and the struggle for women's liberation were seen as inimical largely because black civil rights leaders did not want the white American public to see their demands for full citizenship as synonymous with a radical demand for equality of the sexes. They made black liberation synonymous with gaining full participation in the existing patriarchal nation-state and their demands were for the elimination of racism, not capitalism or patriarchy. Just as white women had publicly disavowed any political connection with black people when they believed that such an alliance was inimical to their interests, black women disassociated themselves from feminist struggle when they were convinced that to appear feminist, i.e. radical, would hurt the cause of black liberation. Black men and women wanted entrance into the mainstream of American life. To gain that entrance they felt it was necessary for them to be conservative.

Black women's organizations, which at one time had concentrated on social services like child care, homes for working women and help for prostitutes, became de-politicized and focused more on social affairs like debutante balls and fundraisers. Black women club members imitated the behavior of middle class white women. Those black women who believed in social equality of the sexes learned to suppress their opinions for fear attention might be shifted from racial issues. They believed they should first support freedom for black people, then later, when that freedom was obtained, work for women's rights. Unfortunately, they did not foresee the strength of black male resistance to the idea that women should have equal status with men.

When the Civil Rights Movement began, black women participated but they did not strive to overshadow black male leaders. When the movement ended, the U.S. public remembered the names of Martin Luther King, Jr., A. Phillip Randolph, and Roy Wilkins but forgot the names of Rosa Parks, Daisy Bates and Fannie Lou Hamer. The 50s leaders of the black civil rights movement, like their 19th century predecessors, made it known that they were eager to establish communities and families using the same pattern as whites. Following the example of white male patriarchs, black men were obsessively concerned with asserting their masculinity while black women imitated the behavior of white women and were obsessive about femininity. An obvious change took place in black sex-role patterns. Black people no longer passively accepted that racial oppression has always forced the black female to be as independent and hardworking as black men; they were demanding that she be more passive, subordinate, and preferably unemployed.

The 50s socialization of black women to assume a more subordinate role in relation to black men occurred as part of an overall effort in the U.S. to brainwash women so as to reverse the effects of World War II. As a result of the war, white and black women had been compelled to be independent, assertive, and hardworking. White men, like black men, wanted to see all women be less assertive, dependent, and unemployed. Mass media was the weapon used to destroy the new-found independence of women. White and black women alike were subjected to endless propaganda which encouraged them to believe that a woman's place was in the home—that her fulfillment in life depended on finding the right man to marry and producing a family. If women were compelled by circumstance to work, they were told that it was better if they didn't compete with men and confined themselves to jobs like teaching and nursing.

The working woman, be she black or white, found it necessary to prove her femininity. Often she developed two demeanors: though she might be assertive and independent on the job, at home she was passive and pleasing. More than ever before in U.S. history, black women were obsessed with pursuing the ideal of femininity described on television, in books and magazines. An emerging black middle class meant that groups of black females had more money than ever before to spend buying fashions, cosmetics, or reading magazines like *McCall's* and *Ladies Home Journal.* Masses of black women who at one time were proud of their ability to work outside the home and yet be good housewives and mothers became discontented with their lot. They wanted only to be housewives and expressed openly their rage and hostility toward black men—a hostility that emerged because they were convinced black men were not striving hard enough to assume the role of sole economic provider in the home so that they could be housewives. Popular sayings of the time like "a black man ain't shit," "the nigger ain't no good," were expressions of black female contempt for black men.

Clearly black women wanted to be in a position to fully participate in the 50s pursuit of "idealized femininity" and resented black men for not aiding them in this quest. They measured black men against a standard set by white males. Since whites defined "achieving manhood" as the ability of a man to be a sole economic provider in a family, many black females tended to regard the black male as a "failed" man. In retaliation, black men openly asserted that they perceived white women as more feminine than black women. Both black females and males were uncertain about their womanhood and manhood. They were both striving to adapt themselves to standards set by the dominant white society. When black women failed for whatever reason to assume a passive subordinate role in relationship to black men, the men became angry. When black men failed to assume the role of sole economic provider in the home, black women were angry.

The tensions and conflicts that emerged in black male/female relationships were dramatized by the 1959 production of Lorraine Hansberry's award-winning play *A Raisin in the Sun.* Conflict prevails in the black male Walter Lee's relationship to his mother and wife. In one scene, as Walter tells his wife Ruth how he intends to spend his mother's insurance money, she refuses to listen; he becomes angry and yells:

Walter: That is just what is wrong with the colored woman in this world... don't understand about building their men up and making 'em feel like they somebody. Like they can do something.

Ruth: There are colored men who do things.

Walter: No thanks to the colored woman.

Ruth: Well, being a colored woman, I guess I can't help myself none.

Walter: We one group of men tied to a race of women with small minds.

The mother in *Raisin in the Sun* is the dominant figure in the home and Walter Lee complains endlessly that she thwarts his assertion of his manhood, that she is a tyrant who forcibly bends him to her will. In the course of the play, Walter Lee is portrayed as irresponsible and unworthy of his mother's trust and respect. She does not respect his assertion of manhood because he acts in an immature manner. However, at the end of the play when he acts in a responsible manner, the mother automatically assumes a subordinate position. The message of the play was twofold. On the one hand, it portrayed the strength and self-sacrificing nature of the single black mother working to ensure the survival of her family, and on the other hand, it stressed the importance of the black male assuming his proper place as patriarch in the home. The mother's way of life is a thing of the past. Walter Lee and Ruth are harbingers of the future. The future black family they portray is the two-parent nuclear set-up wherein man assumes a patriarchal role, the role of decision maker, protector, and upholder of family pride and honor.

Lorraine Hansberry's play was a foretelling of future conflicts between black women and men over the issue of sex-role patterns. This conflict was exaggerated and brought to public attention by the 1965 publication of Danial Moynihan's report *The Negro Family: The Case for National Action*. In his report Moynihan argued that the black American family was being undermined by female dominance. He claimed that racist discrimination against black men in the work force caused black families to have a matriarchal structure which he asserted was out of line with the white American norm, the patriarchal family structure, and that this prevented the black race from being accepted into the mainstream of American life. Moynihan's message was similar to that of black women who admonished black men for not assuming the patriarchal role. The difference in the two perspectives was that Moynihan placed a measure of the responsibility for the black male's inability to assume a patriarchal role on black women, whereas black women felt that racism and black male indifference were the forces that caused black men to reject the role of sole economic provider.

By labeling black women matriarchs, Moynihan implied that those black women who worked and headed households were the enemies of black manhood. Even though Moynihan's supposition that the black family was matriarchal was based on data that showed that only one-fourth of all black families in America were female-headed households, he used this figure to make generalizations about black families as a whole. His generalizations about black family structure, though erroneous, had a tremendous impact upon the black male psyche. Like the American white male in the 50s and 60s, black men were concerned that all women were becoming too assertive and domineering.

The notion that modern women were emasculating men had its origin not in the conflict between black women and black men over sex-role patterns but in the overall conflict in American society over the issue of sex roles. Women as castrator was an image first evoked not in reference to black women and certainly not by Daniel Moynihan; it was popularized by certain psychoanalysts who had their heyday in the 50s. They imposed upon the consciousness of the American public the notion that any career woman, any woman who competed with men, was envious of male power and was likely to be a castrating bitch.

Black women came to be depicted as female castrators par excellence, though not because they were inherently more assertive and independent than white women. History shows that white women were actively competing in the male-dominated power structure long before black women because there was no racial barrier to make entrance into that sphere completely impossible. Black women became the target for many misogynist attacks on female independence largely because of racist scapegoating. Just as the 19th century white public had portrayed black women as embodying all negative traits that were usually attributed to the female sex as a whole while portraying white women as embodying all positive traits, the 20th century white public continued this practice. They idealized and elevated the status of the white female group by debasing and degrading the black female group. Daniel Moynihan did not attempt to document the fact that the so-called "matriarchal" role black women assumed in the female-headed household was the same as the one white women assumed in the female-headed household. Instead, he continued to perpetuate one of the United States' most popular sexist-racist myths about black womanhood—the myth that black women are inherently more assertive, independent, and domineering than white women.

Sexist ideology was the core of the matriarchy myth. Implicit in the assertion that black women were matriarchs was the assumption that patriarchy should be maintained at all costs and that the subordination of the female was necessary for the healthy achievement of manhood. In effect, Moynihan suggested that the negative effects of racist oppression of black people could be eliminated if black females were more passive, subservient and supportive of patriarchy. Once again, woman's liberation was presented as inimical to black liberation.

The extent to which black men absorbed this ideology was made evident in the 60s black liberation movement. Black male leaders of the movement made the liberation of black people from racist oppression synonymous with their gaining the right to assume the role of patriarch, of sexist oppressor. By allowing white men to dictate the terms by which they would define black liberation, black men chose to endorse sexist exploitation and oppression of black women. And in so doing they were compromised. They were not liberated from the system but liberated to serve the system. The movement ended and the system had not changed; it was no less racist or sexist.

Like black men, many black women believed black liberation could only be achieved by the formation of a strong black patriarchy. Many of the black women interviewed in Inez Smith Reid's book *Together Black Women*, published in 1972, openly stated that they felt the role of the female should be a supportive one and that the male ought to be the dominant figure in all black liberation struggles. Typical black female responses were:

> I think the woman should be behind the man. The man should be up first before the woman because Black woman has been over Black man through time in this country. Through no fault of their own they acquired better jobs and better status. They weren't equal to the White men and women but they were above Black men. And now that the revolution is taking place socially I think Black women shouldn't be foremost in the life. I think it should be Black men 'cause men represent the symbol of the races.

or:

> I think a Black female can be one of the greatest assets in the revolution or in the struggle. I think black women have a history of perseverance and strength. I would not like to see that strength turn into domineering tendencies or bossism but I do think we can be that silent strength that the Black man needs to fight the battle for his wife or his woman and his family.

A large number of black women, many who were young, college-educated, and middle class, were seduced in the 60s and 70s by the romanticized concept of idealized womanhood first popularized during the Victorian age. They stressed that woman's role was that of a helpmate to her man. And for the first time in the history of black civil rights movements, black women did not struggle equally with black men. Writing of the 60s black movement in *Black Macho and the Myth of the Superwoman*, Michelle Wallace comments:

> Misogyny was an integral part of Black Macho. Its philosophy, which maintained that black men had been more oppressed than black women, that black women had, in fact, contributed to that oppression, that black men were sexually and morally superior and also exempt from most

of the responsibilities human beings had to other human beings, could only be detrimental to black women. But black women were determined to believe—even as their own guts were telling them it was not so—that they were finally on the verge of liberation from the spectre of the omnipotent blonde with the rosebud lips and the cheese-cake legs. They would no longer have to admire another woman on the pedestal. The pedestal would be theirs. They would no longer have to do their own fighting. They would be fought for. The knight in white armor would ride for them. The beautiful fairy princess would be black.

The women of the Black Movement had little sense of the contradictions in their desire to be models of fragile Victorian womanhood in the midst of revolution. They wanted a house, a picket fence around it, a chicken in the pot, and a man. As they saw it, their only officially desig-nated revolutionary responsibility was to have babies.

Not all black women succumbed to the sexist brainwashing that was so much a part of black liberation rhetoric, but those who did not received no attention. People in the U.S. were fascinated with the image of the black female—strong, fierce, and inde-pendent—meekly succumbing to a passive role, in fact longing to be in a passive role.

Although Angela Davis became a female heroine of the 60s movement, she was admired not for her political commit-ment to the Communist party, not for any of her brilliant analyses of capitalism and racial imperialism, but for her beauty, for her devotion to black men. The American public was not willing to see the "political" Angela Davis; instead they made of her a poster pinup. In general, black people did not approve of her communism and refused to take it seriously. Wallace writes of Angela Davis:

> For all her achievements, she was seen as the epitome of the selfless, sacrificing "good woman"—the only kind of black woman the Movement would accept. She did it for her man, they said. A woman in a woman's place. The so-called political issues were irrelevant.

Contemporary black women who supported patriarchal dominance placed their submission to the status quo in the context of racial politics and argued that they were willing to accept a subordinate role in relationship to black men for the good of the race. They were indeed a new generation of black females—a generation that had been brainwashed not by black revolutionaries but by white society, by the media, to believe that woman's place was in the home. They were the first generation of black women to face competition with white women for the attention of black men. Many of them accepted black male sexism solely because they were afraid of being alone, of not having male companions. The fear of being alone, or of being unloved, had caused women of all races to passively accept sexism and sexist oppression. There was nothing unique or new about the black woman's willingness to accept the sexist-defined female role. The 60s black movement simply became a background in which their acceptance of sexism, or patriarchy, could be announced to the white public that was so convinced that black women were more likely to be assertive and domineering than white women.

Contrary to popular opinion, the sexual politics of the 50s socialized black women to conform to sexist-defined role patterns—not the black macho of the 70s. Black mothers of the 50s had taught their daughters that they should not be proud to work, that they should educate themselves in case they did not find that man who would be the most important force in their lives, who would provide for and protect them. With such a legacy it was not surprising that college-educated black women were embracing patriarchy. The 60s black movement simply exposed a support of sexism and patriarchy that already existed in the black community—it did not create it. Writing of the black woman's response to the 60s civil rights struggle, Michelle Wallace comments:

> The black woman never really dealt with the primary issues of the Black movement. She stopped straightening her hair. She stopped using lighteners and brighteners. She forced herself to be submissive and passive. She preached to her children about the glories of the black man. But then, suddenly, the Black movement was over. Now she has begun to straighten her hair again, to follow the latest fashions in *Vogue* and *Mademoiselle*, to rouge her cheeks furiously, and to speak, not infrequently, of what a dis-

appointment the black man has been. She has little contact with other black women, and if she does, it is not of a deep sort. The discussion is generally of clothes, makeup, furniture, and men. Privately she does whatever she can to stay out of that surplus of black women (one million) who will never find mates. And if she doesn't find a man, she might just decide to have a baby anyway.

Now that an organized black civil rights movement no longer exists, black women do not find it necessary to place their willingness to assume a sexist-defined role in the context of black liberation; so it is much more obvious that their support of patriarchy was not engendered solely by their concern for the black race but by the fact that they live in a culture in which the majority of women support and accept patriarchy.

When the movement toward feminism began in the late 60s, black women rarely participated as a group. Since the dominant white patriarchy and black male patriarchy conveyed to black women the message that to cast a vote in favor of social equality of the sexes, i.e. women's liberation, was to cast a vote against black liberation, they were initially suspicious of the white woman's call for a feminist movement. Many black women refused to participate in the movement because they had no desire to fight against sexism. Theirs was not an unusual stance. The great majority of women in the U.S. did not participate in the women's movement for the same reason. White men were among the first observers of the women's movement to call attention to the absence of black women participants, but they did so solely to mock and ridicule the efforts of white feminists. They smugly questioned the credibility of a women's liberation movement that could not attract women from the most oppressed female groups in American society. They were among the first critics of feminism to raise the question of white female racism. In response, white women liberationists urged black and other non-white women to join their ranks. Those black women who were most vehemently anti-feminist were the most eager to respond. Their stance came to be depicted as *the* black female position on women's liberation. They expressed their views in essays like Ida Lewis' "Women's Rights, Why the Struggle Still Goes On," Linda

LaRue's "Black Liberation and Women's Lib," "Women's Liberation Has No Soul," first published in *Encore* magazine, and Renee Fergueson's "Women's Liberation Has a Different Meaning for Blacks." Linda LaRue's comments on women's liberation were often quoted as if they were the definitive black female response to women's liberation:

> Let it be stated unequivocally that the American white woman has had a better opportunity to live a free and fulfilling life, both mentally and physically, than any other group in the United States, excluding her white husband. Thus any attempt to analogize black oppression with the plight of American white women has all the validity of comparing the neck of a hanging man with the rope-burned hands of an amateur mountain climber.

In their essays, black female anti-feminists revealed hatred and envy of white women. They expended their energy attacking white women liberationists, not by offering any convincing evidence that would support their claim that black women had no need of women's liberation. Black sociologist Joyce Ladner expressed her views on women's liberation in her study of black women *Tomorrow's Tomorrow*:

> Many black women who have traditionally accepted the white models of femininity are now rejecting them for the same general reasons that we should reject the white middle-class lifestyle. Black women in this society are the only ethnic or radical group which has had the opportunity to be women. By this I simply mean that much of the current focus on being liberated from the constraints and protectiveness of the society which is proposed by women's liberation groups has never applied to Black women, and in that sense, we have always been "free," and able to develop as individuals even under the most harsh circumstances. This freedom, as well as the tremendous hardships from which black women suffered, allowed for the development of a personality that is rarely described in the scholarly journals for its obstinate strength and ability to survive. Neither is its peculiar humanistic character and quiet courage viewed as the epitome of what the American model of femininity should be.

Ladner's assertion that black women were "free" became one of the accepted explanations for black female refusal to participate in a women's liberation movement. But such an assertion merely reveals that black women who were most quick to dismiss women's liberation had not thought seriously about feminist struggle. For while white women may have seen feminism as a way to free themselves from the constraints imposed upon them by idealized concepts of femininity, black women could have seen feminism as a way to free themselves from constraints that sexism clearly imposed on their behavior. Only a very naive unenlightened person could confidently state that black women in the U.S. are a liberated female group. The black women who patted themselves on the back for being "already liberated" were really acknowledging their acceptance of sexism and their contentment with patriarchy.

The concentrated focus on black anti-feminist thought was so pervasive that black women who supported feminism and participated in the effort to establish a feminist movement received little attention, if any. For every black anti-feminist article written and published, there existed a pro-feminist black female position. Essays like Cellestine Ware's "Black Feminism," Shirley Chisholm's "Women Must Rebel," Mary Ann Weather's "An Argument for Black Women's Liberation as a Revolutionary Force," and Pauli Murray's "The Liberation of Black Women" all expressed black female support of feminism.

As a group, black women were not opposed to social equality between the sexes but they were not eager to join with white women to organize a feminist movement. The 1972 Virginia Slims American Women's Opinion Poll showed that more black women supported changes in the status of women in society than white women. Yet their support of feminist issues did not lead them as a collective group to actively participate in the women's liberation movement. Two explanations are usually given to explain their lack of participation. The first is that the 60s black movement encouraged black women to assume a subservient role and caused them to reject feminism. The second is that black women were, as one white woman liberationist put it, "repelled by the racial and class composition of the women's movement." Taken at face value these reasons seem adequate. Examined in a historical context in which black women have rallied in support of women's rights despite pressure from black men to assume a subordinate position, and despite the fact that white middle and upper class women have dominated every women's movement in the U.S., they seem inadequate. While they do provide justification for the anti-feminist black female position, they do not explain why black women who support feminist ideology refuse to participate fully in the contemporary women's movement.

Initially, black feminists approached the women's movement white women had organized eager to join the struggle to end sexist oppression. We were disappointed and disillusioned when we discovered that white women in the movement had little knowledge of or concern for the problems of lower class and poor women or the particular problems of non-white women from all classes. Those of us who were active in women's groups found that white feminists lamented the absence of large numbers of non-white participants but were unwilling to change the movement's focus so that it would better address the needs of women from all classes and races. Some white women even argued that groups not represented by a numerical majority could not expect their concerns to be given attention. Such a position reinforced the black female participants' suspicion that white participants wanted the movement to concentrate on the concerns not of women as a collective group, but on the individual concerns of the small minority who had organized the movement.

Black feminists found that sisterhood for most white women did not mean surrendering allegiance to race, class, and sexual preference, to bond on the basis of the shared political belief that a feminist revolution was necessary so that all people, especially women, could reclaim their rightful citizenship in the world. From our peripheral position in the movement we saw that the potential radicalism of feminist ideology was being undermined by women who, while paying lip service to revolutionary goals, were primarily concerned with gaining entrance into the capitalist patriarchal power structure. Although white feminists denounced the white male, calling him an imperialist, capitalist, sexist, racist pig, they made women's liberation synonymous with women obtaining the right to fully participate in the very system they identified as oppressive. Their anger was not merely a response to sexist oppression. It was an expression of their jealousy and envy of white men who held positions of power in the system while they were denied access to those positions. Individual black feminists despaired as we witnessed the appropriation of feminist ideology by elitist, racist white women. We were unable to usurp leadership positions within the movement so that we could spread an authentic message of feminist revolution. We could not even get a hearing at women's groups because they were organized and controlled by white women. Along with politically aware white women, we, black feminists, began to feel that no organized feminist struggle really existed. We dropped out of groups, weary of hearing talk about women as a force that could change the world when we had not changed ourselves. Some black women formed "black feminist" groups which resembled in almost every way the groups they had left. Others struggled alone. Some of us continued to go to organizations, women's studies classes, or conferences, but were not fully participating.

For ten years now I have been an active feminist. I have been working to destroy the psychology of dominance that permeates Western culture and shapes female/male sex roles and I have advocated reconstruction of U.S. society based on human rather than material values. I have been a student in women's studies classes, a participant in feminist seminars, organizations, and various women's groups. Initially I believed that the women who were active in feminist activities were concerned about sexist oppression and its impact on women as a collective group. But I became disillusioned as I saw various groups of women appropriating feminism to serve their own opportunistic ends. Whether it was women university professors crying sexist oppression (rather than sexist discrimination) to attract attention to their efforts to gain promotion; or women using feminism to mask their sexist attitudes; or women writers superficially exploring feminist themes to advance their own careers, it was evident that eliminating sexist oppression was not the primary concern. While their rallying cry was sexist oppression, they showed little concern about the status of women as a collective group in our society. They were primarily interested in making feminism a forum for the expression of their own self-centered needs and desires. Not once did they entertain the possibility that their concerns might not represent the concerns of oppressed women.

Even as I witnessed the hypocricy of feminists, I clung to the hope that increased participation of women from different races and classes in feminist activities would lead to a re-evaluation of feminism, radical reconstruction of feminist ideology, and the launching of a new movement that would more adequately address the concerns of both women and men. I was not willing to see white women feminists as "enemies." Yet as I moved from one women's group to another trying to offer a different perspective, I met with hostility and resentment. White women liberationists saw feminism as "their" movement and resisted any efforts by non-white women to critique, challenge, or change its direction.

During this time, I was struck by the fact that the ideology of feminism, with its emphasis on transforming and changing the social structure of the U.S., in no way resembled the actual reality of American feminism. Largely because feminists themselves, as they attempted to take feminism beyond the realm of radical rhetoric into the sphere of American life, revealed that they remained imprisoned in the very structures they hoped to change. Consequently, the sisterhood we talked about has not become a reality. And the women's movement we envisioned would have a transformative effect on U.S. culture has not emerged. Instead, the hierarchical pattern of sex-race relationships already established by white capitalist patriarchy merely assumed a different form under feminism. Women liberationists did not invite a wholistic analysis of woman's status in society that would take into consideration the varied aspects of our experience. In their eagerness to promote the idea of sisterhood, they ignored the complexity of woman's experience. While claiming to liberate women from biological determinism, they denied women an existence outside that determined by our sexuality. It did not serve the interest of upper and middle class white feminists to discuss race and class.

Consequently, much feminist literature, while providing meaningful information concerning women's experiences, is both racist and sexist in its content. I say this not to condemn or dismiss. Each time I read a feminist book that is racist and sexist, I feel a sadness and an anguish of spirit. For to know that there thrives in the very movement that has claimed to liberate women endless snares that bind us tighter and tighter to old oppressive ways is to witness the failure of yet another potentially radical, transformative movement in our society.

Although the contemporary feminist movement was initially motivated by the sincere desire of women to eliminate sexist oppression, it takes place within the framework of a larger, more powerful cultural system that encourages women and men to place the fulfillment of individual aspirations above their desire for collective change. Given this framework, it is not surprising that feminism has been undermined by the narcissism, greed, and individual opportunism of its leading exponents. A feminist ideology that mouths radical rhetoric about resistance and revolution while actively seeking to establish itself within the capitalist patriarchal system is essentially corrupt. While the contemporary feminist movement has successfully stimulated an awareness of the impact of sexist discrimination on the social status of women in the U.S., it has done little to eliminate sexist oppression. Teaching women how to defend themselves against male rapists is not the same as working to change society so that men will not rape. Establishing houses for battered women does not change the psyches of the men who batter them, nor does it change the culture that promotes and condones their brutality. Attacking heterosexuality does little to strengthen the self-concept of the masses of women who desire to be with men. Denouncing housework as menial labor does not restore to the woman houseworker the pride and dignity in her labor she is stripped of by patriarchal devaluation. Demanding an end to institutionalized sexism does not ensure an end to sexist oppression.

The rhetoric of feminism with its emphasis on resistance, rebellion, and revolution created an illusion of militancy and radicalism that masked the fact that feminism was in no way a challenge or a threat to capitalist patriarchy. To perpetuate the notion that all men are creatures of privilege with access to a personal fulfillment and a personal liberation denied women, as feminists do, is to lend further credibility to the sexist mystique of male power that proclaims all that is male is inherently superior to that which is female. A feminism so rooted in envy, fear, and idealization of male power cannot expose the de-humanizing effect of sexism on men and women in American society. Today, feminism offers women not liberation but the right to act as surrogate men. It has not provided a blueprint for change that would lead to the elimination of sexist oppression or a transformation of our society. The women's movement has become a kind of ghetto or concentration camp for women who are seeking to attain the kind of power they feel men have. It provides a forum for the expression of their feelings of anger, jealousy, rage, and disappointment with men. It provides an atmosphere where women who have little in common, who may resent or even feel indifferent to one another can bond on the basis of shared negative feelings toward men. Finally, it gives women of all races, who desire to assume the imperialist, sexist, racist positions of destruction men hold with a platform that allows them to act as if the attainment of their personal aspirations and their lust for power is for the common good of all women.

Right now, women in the U.S. are witnessing the demise of yet another women's rights movement. The future of collective feminist struggle is bleak. The women who appropriated feminism to advance their own opportunistic causes have achieved their desired ends and are no longer interested in feminism as a political ideology. Many women who remain active in women's rights groups and organizations stubbornly refuse to critique the distorted analysis of woman's lot in society popularized by women's liberation. Since these women are not oppressed they can support a feminist movement that is reformist, racist, and classist because they see no urgent need for radical change. Although women in the U.S. have come closer to obtaining social equality with men, the capitalist-patriarchal system is unchanged. It is still imperialist, racist, sexist, and oppressive.

The recent women's movement failed to adequately address the issue of sexist oppression, but that failure does not change the fact that it exists, that we are victimized by it to varying degrees, nor does it free any of us from assuming responsibility for change. Many black women are daily victimized by sexist oppression. More often than not we bear our pain in silence, patiently waiting for a change to come. But neither passive acceptance nor stoic endurance lead to change. Change occurs only when there is action, movement, revolution. The 19th century black female was a woman of action. Her suffering, the harshness of her lot in a racist, sexist world, and her concern for the plight of others motivated her to join feminist struggle. She did not allow the racism of white women's rights advocates or the sexism of black men to deter her from political involvement. She did not rely on any group to provide her with a blueprint for change. She was a maker of blueprints. In an address given before an audience of women in 1892 Anna Cooper proudly voiced the black woman's perspective on feminism:

> Let woman's claim be as broad in the concrete as in the abstract. We take our stand on the solidarity of humanity, the oneness of life, and the unnaturalness and injustice of all special favoritism, whether of sex, race, country, or condition. If one link of the chain is broken, the chain is broken. A bridge is no stronger than its weakest part, and a cause is not worthier than its weakest element. Least of all can woman's cause afford to decry the weak. We want, then, as toilers for the universal triumph of justice and human rights, to go to our homes from this Congress demanding an entrance not through a gateway for ourselves, our race, our sex, or our sect, but a grand highway for humanity. The colored woman feels that woman's cause is one and universal; and that not till the image of God whether in parian or ebony, is sacred and inviolable; not till race, color, sex, and condition are seen as accidents, and not the substance of life; not till the universal title of humanity to life, liberty, and the pursuit of happiness is conceded to be inalienable to all; not till then is woman's cause won— not the white woman's, nor the black woman's, nor the red woman's, but the cause of every man and of every woman who has writhed silently under a mighty wrong. Woman's

> wrongs are thus indissolubly linked with all undefended
> woe, and the acquirement of her "rights" will mean the
> final triumph of all right over might, the supremacy of the
> moral forces of reason, and justice, and love in the
> government of the nations of earth.

Cooper spoke for herself and thousands of other black women
who had been born into slavery, who because they had been
severely victimized, felt a compassion and a concern for the
plight of all oppressed peoples. Had all women's rights
advocates shared their sentiments the feminist movement in
the U.S. would be truly radical and transformative.

Feminism is an ideology in the making. According to the
Oxford English Dictionary the term "feminism" was first used
in the latter part of the 19th century and it was defined as
having the "qualities of females." The meaning of the term has
been gradually transformed and the 20th century dictionary
definition of feminism is a "theory of the political, economic,
and social equality of the sexes." To many women this
definition is inadequate. In the introduction to *The Remembered Gate: Origins of American Feminism* Barbara Berg
defines feminism as a "broad movement embracing numerous
phases of woman's emancipation." She further states:

> It is the freedom to decide her own destiny; freedom from
> sex-determined role; freedom from society's oppressive
> restrictions; freedom to express her thoughts fully and to
> convert them freely to actions. Feminism demands the
> acceptance of woman's right to individual conscience and
> judgment. It postulates that woman's essential worth
> stems from her common humanity and does not depend on
> the other relationships of her life.

Her expanded definition of feminism is useful but limited.
Many women have found that neither the struggle for "social
equality" nor the focus on an "ideology of woman as an autono-
mous being" are enough to rid society of sexism and male
domination. To me feminism is not simply a struggle to end
male chauvinism or a movement to ensure that women will
have equal rights with men; it is a commitment to eradicating
the ideology of domination that permeates Western culture on
various levels—sex, race, and class, to name a few—and a

commitment to reorganizing U.S. society so that the self-development of people can take precedence over imperialism, economic expansion, and material desires. Writers of a feminist pamphlet published anonymously in 1976 urged women to develop political consciousness:

> In all these struggles we must be assertive and challenging, combating the deep-seated tendency in Americans to be liberal, that is, to evade struggling over questions of principle for fear of creating tensions or becoming unpopular. Instead we must live by the fundamental dialectical principle: that progress comes only from struggling to resolve contradictions.

It is a contradiction that white females have structured a women's liberation movement that is racist and excludes many non-white women. However, the existence of that contradiction should not lead any woman to ignore feminist issues. Oftentimes I am asked by black women to explain why I would call myself a feminist and by using that term ally myself with a movement that is racist. I say, "The question we must ask again and again is how can racist women call themselves feminists." It is obvious that many women have appropriated feminism to serve their own ends, especially those white women who have been at the forefront of the movement; but rather than resigning myself to this appropriation I choose to re-appropriate the term "feminism," to focus on the fact that to be "feminist" in any authentic sense of the term is to want for all people, female and male, liberation from sexist role patterns, domination, and oppression.

Today masses of black women in the U.S. refuse to acknowledge that they have much to gain by feminist struggle. They fear feminism. They have stood in place so long that they are afraid to move. They fear change. They fear losing what little they have. They are afraid to openly confront white feminists with their racism or black males with their sexism, not to mention confronting white men with their racism and sexism. I have sat in many a kitchen and heard black women express a belief in feminism and eloquently critique the women's movement explaining their refusal to participate. I have witnessed their refusal to express these same views in a public setting. I know their fear exists because they have seen us trampled upon, raped, abused, slaughtered, ridiculed and mocked. Only a few black women have rekindled the spirit of feminist struggle that stirred the hearts and minds of our 19th century sisters. We, black women who advocate feminist ideology, are pioneers. We are clearing a path for ourselves and our sisters. We hope that as they see us reach our goal—no longer victimized, no longer unrecognized, no longer afraid— they will take courage and follow.

Selected Bibliography

American Anti-Slavery Society, *American Slavery As It Is: Testimony of a Thousand Witnesses*. New York, 1839.

Andreski, Iris, *Old Wive's Tales*. London: Routledge and Kegan Paul, 1970.

Aptheker, Herbert, *A Documentary History of the Negro People in the United States*. New York, 1951.

Babcox, Deborah and Madeline Belkin, *Liberation Now*. New York: Dell, 1971.

Bancroft, Frederic, *Slave Trading in the Old South*. Baltimore: J.H. First Company, 1931.

Baraka, Imamu Amiri, "Black Women," in *Black World*, 1970.

Barber, Benjamin, *Liberating Feminism*. New York: Delta, 1976.

Bennett, Lerone, *Before the Mayflower*. Baltimore: Penguin, 1966.

————, *Pioneers in Protest*. Baltimore: Penguin, 1969.

Benton, Myron, *The American Male*. New York: Coward-McCann, Inc., 1966.

Berg, Barbara, *The Remembered Gate: Origins of American Feminism*. New York: Oxford University Press, 1979.

Berlin, Ira, *Slaves Without Masters*. New York: Vintage Books, 1976.

Bernard, Jessie, *The Future of Marriage*. New York: Bantam, 1973.

————, *Marriage and Family Among Negroes*. New Jersey: Prentice Hall, 1966.

Billington, Ray, ed., *Journal of Charlotte Forten*. New York: Collier, 1961.

Billingsly, Andrew, *Black Families in White America*. Englewood Cliffs, New Jersey: Prentice Hall, 1968.

Bird, Caroline, *Born Female*. New York: Pocket Books, 1968.

Bogin, Ruth and Bert Lowenberg, *Black Women in Nineteenth-Century American Life*. Pennsylvania: Pennsylvania State Univ. Press, 1976.

Botkin, B.A., *Lay My Burden Down*. Chicago: University of Chicago Press, 1945.

Brotz, Howard, ed., *Negro Social and Political Thought, 1850-1920*. New York: Basic Books, 1966.

Brownmiller, Susan, *Against Our Will*. New York: Simon and Schuster, 1975.

Cade, Toni, ed., *The Black Woman*. New York: Signet, 1970.

Carmichael, Stokely and Charles Hamilton, *Black Power*. New York: Vintage Books, 1967.

Cash, W.J. *The Mind of the South*. New York: Vintage, 1941.

Chafe, William, *Women and Equality*. New York: Oxford University Press, 1977.

Child, Lydia Maria, *Brief History of the Condition of Women*. New York: C.S. Francis and Co., 1854.

————, *An Appeal in Favor of Americans Called Africans*, reprint. New York: Arno Press, 1968.

Chisholm, Shirley, "Racism and Anti-Feminism," in *The Black Scholar*, pp. 40-45, 1970.

Clarke, Jessie, *A New Day for the Colored Woman Worker*. New York, 1919.

Coles, Jane and Robert, *Women of Crisis*. New York: Dell, 1978.

Cooper, Anna Julia, *A Voice from the South*. Xenia, Ohio, 1892.

Cott, Nancy, *Bonds of Womanhood*. New Haven: Yale University Press, 1977.

Cudlipp, Edythe, *Understanding Women's Liberation*. New York: Paperback Library, 1971.

Day, Caroline Bond, *A Study of Some Negro-White Families in the U.S.* Connecticut: Negro University Press, 1970.

Daly, Mary, *Gyn/Ecology*. Boston: Beacon Press, 1978.

Davis, Angela, *An Autobiography*. New York: Random House, 1974.

————, "Reflections on the Black Woman's Role in the Community of Slaves," in *The Black Scholar*, Vol. 3, Number 4, December 1971.

Deckard, Barbara, *The Women's Movement*. New York: Harper and Row, 1975.

Diner, Helen, *Mothers and Amazons*. New York: Anchor Press, 1973.

Doherty, Joseph, *Moral Problems of Interracial Marriage*. Washington: Catholic University of America Press, 1949.

Doughtery, Molly, *Becoming a Woman in Rural Black Culture*. New York: Holt, Rinehart, and Winston. 1978.

Douglass, Frederick, *Narrative of the Life of Frederick Douglass*. Edited by Benjamin Quarles. Cambridge, Mass.: Belknap Press, 1969.

Douglas, Mary, *Purity and Danger*. New York: Praeger, 1966.

Draper, Theodore, *The Rediscovery of Black Nationalism*. New York: Viking Press, 1969.

Drimmer, Melvin, *Black History*. New York: Doubleday, 1968.

Duniway, Abigail Scott, *Path Breaking*. New York: Shocken Books, 1971.

Eastman, Crystal, *On Women and Revolution*. Edited by Blanche Cook. New York: Oxford University Press, 1978.

Eisenstein, Zillah, ed., *Capitalist Patriarchy and the Case for Socialist Feminism*. New York: Monthly Review Press, 1979.

Elkins, Stanley, *Slavery*. New York: Universal Library, 1963.

Fasteau, Marc, *The Male Machine*. New York: Delta, 1975.

Feldstein, Stanley, *Once a Slave*. New York: William Morrow and Company, 1971.

Figes, Eva, *Patriarchal Attitudes*. Greenwich, Conn.: Fawcett Press, 1970.

Firestone, Shulamith, *The Dialectic of Sex*. New York: Bantam, 1970.

Flexner, Eleanor, *Century of Struggle*. New York: Atheneum, 1970.

————, *Mary Wollenscraft*. Maryland: Penguin, 1972.

Frazier, E. Franklin, *Black Bourgeoisie*. New York: Collier, 1962.

Freeman, Jo, *The Politics of Women's Liberation*. New York: David McKay Co., 1975.

Genovese, Eugene, *Roll, Jordan, Roll*. New York: Vintage Press, 1976.

————, *The World the Slaveholders Made*. New York: Vintage Press, 1977.

Ginzberg, Eli, *Educated American Women*. New York: Columbia University Press, 1966.

Gordon, Albert, *Intermarriage: Interfaith, Interracial, Interethnic*. Boston: Beacon Press, 1964.

Gornick, Vivian and Barbara Moran, *Women in Sexist Society*. New York: Basic Books, 1971.

Greer, Germaine, *The Female Eunuch*. New York: Bantam Books, 1971.

Grier, William and Price Cobbs, *Black Rage*. New York: Bantam Books, 1968.

————, *The Jesus Bag*. New York: Bantam Books, 1971.

Griffiths, Mattie, *Autobiography of a Female Slave*. New York: Redfield, 1857.

Gutman, Herbert, *The Black Family in Slavery and Freedom*. New York: Vintage Books, 1977.

Hafkin, Nancy and Edna Bay, *Women in Africa*. Palo Alto, Calif.: Stanford University Press, 1976.

Halsell, Grace, *Black-White Sex*. Connecticut: Fawcett, 1972.

————, *Soul Sister*. Connecticut: Fawcett, 1969.

Hansberry, Lorraine, *To Be Young, Gifted and Black*. New York: Signet Books, 1970.

Harley, Sharon and Rosalyn Terborg-Penn, *The Afro-American Woman*. New York: Kennikat Press, 1978.

Hernton, Calvin, *Sex and Racism in America*. New York: Grove, 1965.

Isaacs, Harold, *The New World of Negro Americans*. New York: Viking Press, 1963.

Janeway, Elizabeth, *Man's World, Woman's Place*. New York: Delta, 1971.

Jones, Leroi, *Home*. New York: William Morrow, 1966.

————, *Raise, Race, Rays, Raze*. New York: Vintage Press, 1972.

Kemble, Francis, *Journal of a Residence on a Georgian Plantation in 1783-1839*. Edited by John Scott. New York: Signet Books, 1975.

Koedt, Anne, ed., *Radical Feminism.* New York: Quadrangle Books, 1973.

Kraditor, Aileen, ed., *Up From the Pedestal.* Chicago: Quadrangle, 1968.

Ladner, Joyce. *Tomorrow's Tomorrow.* New York: Anchor Books, 1972.

Lerner, Gerda, *Black Women in White America.* New York: Vintage Press, 1973.

Lincoln, C. Eric, *The Black Muslims in America.* Boston: Beacon Press, 1961.

Logan, Rayford, *The Betrayal of the Negro.* New York: Collier, 1954.

Meltzer, Milton, *Slavery from the Rise of Western Civilization to Today.* New York: Dell, 1971.

Millett, Kate, *Sexual Politics.* New York: Avon, 1971.

Milner, Christina and Richard Milner, *Black Players.* Boston: Little Brown and Co., 1972.

Morgan, Robin, ed., *Sisterhood Is Powerful.* New York: Vintage Press, 1970.

Myrdal, Gunnar, *An American Dilemma.* New York: Harper and Brothers, 1944.

Nichols, Charles, *Black Men in Chains.* New York: Lawrence Hill, 1972.

Paulme, Denise, ed., *Women of Tropical Africa.* Berkeley: University of California Press, 1963.

Quarles, Benjamin, *The Negro in the Making of America.* New York: Collier, 1964.

Reid, Inez, *Together Black Women.* New York: Third Press, 1975.

Reiter, Rayna, ed., *Toward an Anthropology of Women.* New York: Monthly Review Press, 1975.

Riegel, Robert, *American Feminists.* Kansas: University of Kansas Press, 1963.

Rogers, Katherine, *The Troublesome Helpmate.* Seattle: University of Washington Press, 1966.

Scott, Anne, *The Southern Lady, From Pedestal to Politics, 1830-1930.* Chicago: University of Chicago Press.

Seifer, Nancy, ed., *Nobody Speaks For Me.* New York: Simon and Schuster, 1976.

Sinclair, Andrew, *The Emancipation of the American Woman.* New York: Harper-Colophon, 1965.

Silberman, Charles, *Crisis in Black and White*. New York: Vintage Press, 1964.

Smith, Page, *Daughters of the Promised Land*. Boston: Little, Brown and Co., 1970.

Smuts, Robert, *Women and Work in America*. New York: Schoken Books, 1971.

Snodgrass, Jon, ed., *For Men Against Sexism*. Albion, Calif.: Times Change Press, 1977.

Sochen, June, *Herstory*. New York: Alfred Publishing Co., 1974.

————, *The New Woman in Greenwich Village, 1910-1920*. New York: Quadrangle Books, 1972.

Spears, John, American Slave Trade. New York: Kennikat Press. First printed in 1900.

Spruill, Julia, *Women's Life and Work in the Southern Colonies*. New York: W.W. Norton, 1972.

Stambler, Sookie, ed., *Women's Liberation: Blueprint for the Future*. New York: Ace Books, 1970.

Stampp, Kenneth, *The Peculiar Institution*. New York: Vintage Press, 1956.

Staples, Robert, *The Black Woman in America*. Chicago: Nelson Hill, 1973.

Tanner, Leslie, ed., *Voices From Women's Liberation*. New York: Mentor, 1970.

Thompson, Mary, ed., *Voices of the New Feminism*. Boston: Beacon Press, 1970.

Vilar, Esther, *The Manipulated Man*. New York: Farra, Strauss, and Giroux, 1972.

Wallace, Michele, *Black Macho and the Myth of the Super Woman*. New York: Dial Press, 1978.

Ware, Cellestine, *Woman Power*. New York: Tower Publications, 1970.

Washington, Joseph, *Marriage in Black and White*. Boston: Beacon Press, 1970.

Williams, Eric, *Capitalism and Slavery*. New York: Capricorn, 1966.

Woodward, C. Vann, *The Strange Career of Jim Crow*. New York: Oxford University Press, 1957.

Index